BLUE 10
EXORCIST
KAZUE KATO

Contents 10

Cast of Characters

Rin Okumura

Born of a human mother and Satan, the God of Demons, Rin Okumura has powers he can barely control. After Satan kills Father Fujimoto, Rin's foster father, Rin decides to become an Exorcist so he can someday defeat Satan. Now a first-year student at True Cross Academy and an Exwire at the Exorcism Cram School, he hopes to someday become a Knight. When he draws the Koma Sword, he manifests his infernal power in the form of blue flames. He succeeded in defeating the Impure King and affirmed his determination to live with his flame.

Yukio Okumura

Rin's brother. Hoping to become a doctor, he's a genius who is the youngest student ever to become an instructor at the Exorcism Cram School. An instructor in Demon Pharmaceuticals, he possesses the titles of Doctor and Dragoon. Todo told him that his true nature is that of a demon.

Shiemi Moriyama

Daughter of the owner of Futsumaya, an Exorcist supply shop. Inspired by Rin and Yukio, she became an Exwire and hopes to someday become an Exorcist. She possesses the ability to become a Tamer and can summon a baby Greenman named Nee.

Ryuji Suguro

Heir to the venerable Buddhist sect known as Myodha in Kyoto. He is an Exwire who hopes to become an Exorcist someday so he can reestablish his family's temple, which fell on hard times after the Blue Night. He wants to achieve the titles of Dragoon and Aria.

Shima Renzo

Once a pupil of Suguro's father and now Suguro's friend. He's an Exwire who wants to become an Aria. He has an easygoing personality and is totally girl-crazy.

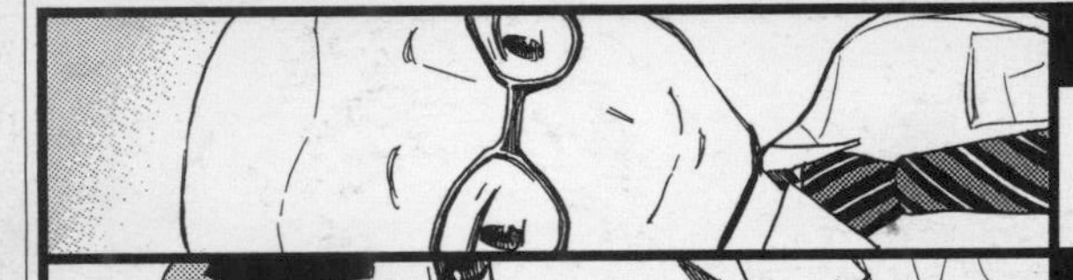

Miwa Konekomaru

Like Shima, he was once a pupil of Suguro's father and is now Suguro's friend. He's an Exwire who hopes to become an Exorcist someday. He is small in size and has a quiet and composed personality.

Izumo Kamiki

An Exwire with the blood of shrine maidens. She has the ability to become a Tamer and can summon two white foxes.

Noriko Paku

An old friend of Kamiki's. They entered the Exorcism Cram School together, but she couldn't keep up with classes and dropped out. She is currently attending regular classes at True Cross Academy High School.

Nemu Takara

A student at the Exorcism Cram School. He rarely speaks, but sometime he uses ventriloquism with a puppet he carries around. Mephisto played a role in his acceptance to True Cross Academy.

Shura Kirigakure

An upper-rank special investigator dispatched by Vatican Headquarters to True Cross Academy. A Senior Exorcist First Class who holds the titles of Knight, Tamer, Doctor and Aria.She used to be Father Fujimoto's pupil.

Mephisto Pheles

President of True Cross Academy and head of the Exorcism Cram School. He was Father Fujimoto's friend, and now he is Rin and Yukio's guardian. He plans to turn Rin into a weapon for use in the fight against Satan.

AMAIMON

Mephisto Pheles's younger brother. A ruler in Gehenna who bears the title King of Earth. Ever since he almost lost to Rin in battle, he's been obsessed with him.

ARTHUR A. ANGEL

A Senior Exorcist First Class and the current Paladin. He wields the demon sword Caliban and is certain that Rin, who has Satan's blood, should be destroyed.

SABUROTA TODO

He comes from an honorable family that has supplied the Order with Exorcists for generations. However, he has joined the demons and awakened the Impure King. Since a fight with Yukio, he has been in hiding.

KINZO SHIMA

The fourth son of the Shima family. An Intermediate Buddhist Exorcist Second Class holding the classifications of Knight and Aria. He's short-tempered and always ready for a fight.

SHIRO FUJIMOTO

The man who raised Rin and Yukio. He was a priest at True Cross Cathedral. He held the rank of Paladin and once taught Demon Pharmaceuticals. Satan possessed him and he gave his life defending Rin.

KURO

A Cat Sídhe who was once Shiro's familiar. After Shiro's death, he began turning back into a demon. Rin saved him, and now the two are practically inseparable. His favorite drink is the catnip wine Shiro used to make.

THE STORY SO FAR

UNKNOWN TO RIN OKUMURA, BOTH HUMAN AND DEMON BLOOD RUNS IN HIS VEINS. IN AN ARGUMENT WITH HIS FOSTER FATHER, FATHER FUJIMOTO, RIN LEARNS THAT SATAN IS HIS TRUE FATHER. SATAN SUDDENLY APPEARS AND TRIES TO DRAG RIN DOWN TO GEHENNA BECAUSE RIN HAS INHERITED HIS POWER. FATHER FUJIMOTO FIGHTS TO DEFEND RIN, BUT DIES IN THE PROCESS. RIN DECIDES TO BECOME AN EXORCIST SO HE CAN SOMEDAY DEFEAT SATAN AND BEGINS STUDYING AT THE EXORCISM CRAM SCHOOL UNDER THE INSTRUCTION OF HIS TWIN BROTHER YUKIO, WHO IS ALREADY AN EXORCIST.

ONE DAY, THEY LEARN THAT SOMEONE HAS STOLEN THE LEFT EYE OF THE IMPURE KING FROM THE ACADEMY'S DEEP KEEP.

RIN AND THE OTHERS GO TO THE KYOTO FIELD OFFICE OF THE KNIGHTS OF THE TRUE CROSS TO ASSIST DEFENSE OF THE RIGHT EYE OF THE IMPURE KING. TODO, A FORMER EXORCIST, WHO STOLE THE LEFT EYE, AWAKENS THE IMPURE KING.

AFTER RIN'S FLAME RAGES OUT OF CONTROL, HE LOSES HIS CONFIDENCE AND THE ABILITY TO DRAW THE KOMA SWORD. BUT IN RESPONSE TO SUGURO'S FAITH IN HIM, HE IS ABLE TO DRAW HIS SWORD AGAIN. THEN, BORROWING STRENGTH FROM AN UCCHUSMA AND WIELDING FLAME, HE SUCCEEDS IN DEFEATING THE IMPURE KING.

MEANWHILE, YUKIO FIGHTS TODO, AND AS THE BATTLE AROUND THEM RAGES, HE SENSES THAT HE HAS THE SAME FIRE IN HIS OWN EYES AS HIS BROTHER. AFRAID, HE KEEPS IT A SECRET.

BEFORE RETURNING TO TRUE CROSS ACADEMY, THE STUDENTS GO ON A MISSION TO EXORCISE A KRAKEN, AND RIN AFFIRMS HIS DETERMINATION TO LIVE TOGETHER WITH HIS FLAME. HE ASKS YUKIO TO ACCEPT HIS FLAME AS WELL, AND THE TWO CLASH. IN THE END, RIN REALIZES THAT YUKIO'S RELUCTANCE IS OUT OF WORRY FOR HIM SINCE THEY ARE BROTHERS WHO HAVE NO OTHER FAMILY. TOGETHER, WITH SHIEMI, WHO HAS GROWN IN STRENGTH, THEY COOPERATE IN BATTLE AND DEFEAT THE KRAKEN!

HOWEVER, YUKIO INCREASINGLY FEELS AS IF RIN IS SHOWING HIM UP, AND NOW HE CARRIES A DREAD SECRET WITHIN...

Chapter 38: Exorcist

Where am I?

CHIRP
CHIRP
JAPAN: TRUE CROSS ACADEMY TOWN
TRUE CROSS ACADEMY PRIVATE HIGH SCHOOL

EXORCIST:

A PRIEST OR MEMBER OF THE KNIGHTS OF THE TRUE CROSS WHO EXPELS DEMONS POSSESSING A PERSON OR THING.

THE KNIGHTS OF THE TRUE CROSS ARE A MILITANT GROUP STEMMING FROM THE MILITARY ORDERS OF THE MEDIEVAL CATHOLIC CHURCH.

AS THE ORGANIZATION GREW AND BEGAN FIGHTING DEMONS ALL OVER THE WORLD, IT ADOPTED INDIGENOUS METHODS OF EXORCISM.

IN MODERN TIMES, IT ADDRESSES ALL MANNER OF DEMONS REGARDLESS OF FAITH OR CULTURE.

KNIGHT
RIGHT
GRSADE
BELLUM
FATUM
VITA MORI

IT IS THE WORLD'S LARGEST EXORCIST ORGANIZATION.

MUTTER
BUT MOST PEOPLE NO LONGER BELIEVE IN DEMONS.
MUTTER
THEY THINK OF EXORCISTS AS SHAMANS OR COUNSELORS.
CHATTER
CHATTER
TAKE YOUR SEATS, EVERYONE!
TIME TO TAKE ATTENDANCE!
ECHIZEN?
HERE.
HMM
HMM
WHEN I COULDN'T SEE THEM, I DIDN'T BELIEVE EITHER.
MY FIRST EXORCIST
Easy to read!
OKUMURA?
BUT IF EVERYONE COULD SEE THEM...
HERE.

...THEY WOULD BE PANICKING RIGHT NOW.
GLORK ... GLORK-
HISHIGAE?
HERE.

WHAT'S THE MATTER, MR. GODAIIN?
UH...
...I...
...I JUST...
I...
I THINK I WAS D-DREAMING OR SOMETHING...
SNICKER
SNICKER
SNICKER
HMPH!
GET YOUR HEAD OUT OF SUMMER VACATION MODE!

GAH
GLORK...
...LORK...
SHLLL
FWIK
VEEN
GLORK-LORK-LORK...
UF
WHAP
!!
GODAIIN!!
That's your name, right?
DON'T MAKE EYE CONTACT.

OKU...
...MURA?
!
CAN...
CAN *YOU* SEE THAT TOO?!
YEAH.
YOU CAN JUST IGNORE THAT TYPE.
SEE YA.

I THOUGHT I WAS GOING CRAZY!
WHAT'S GOING ON?
WHY ARE WE THE ONLY ONES WHO CAN SEE THEM?
OTHERS CAN SEE THEM TOO.
REALLY?!
BY THE WAY...
IF HE CAN SEE DEMONS...
*...THEN HE MUST HAVE **TEMPTAINT.***

...DID SOMETHING HAPPEN TO YOU JUST BEFORE YOU STARTED SEEING THEM?
LIKE AN INJURY OR SOMETHING?
?
NO, NOT RECENTLY...
THAT'S STRANGE.
OR MAYBE YOU JUST DIDN'T NOTICE.
BUT COME TO THINK OF IT...

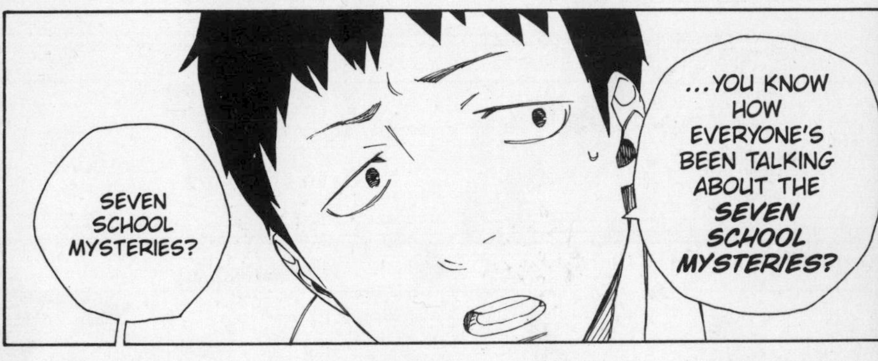
...YOU KNOW HOW EVERYONE'S BEEN TALKING ABOUT THE *SEVEN SCHOOL MYSTERIES?*
SEVEN SCHOOL MYSTERIES?
EVER SINCE SUMMER VACATION ENDED...
...LOTS OF PEOPLE SAY THEY'VE EXPERIENCED THEM.
THAT'S ABOUT WHEN I STARTED SEEING THINGS.
HMM...
?
HOW ABOUT *YOU*, OKUMURA?

HM?

OH, ME?

I'M AN EXORCIST-IN-TRAINING.

HUH?!

YOU ARE?!

SO... ...DOES THAT MEAN...

...TH-THAT THING IS A *DEMON*?!

YEAH. THAT'S WHAT WE CALL THEM, ANYWAY.

A WHOLE OTHER WORLD EXISTS...

IT'S LIKE A BAD DREAM.

IT'S HARD TO SWALLOW ALL AT ONCE.

THANK YOU.
YOU'RE A GOOD GUY!

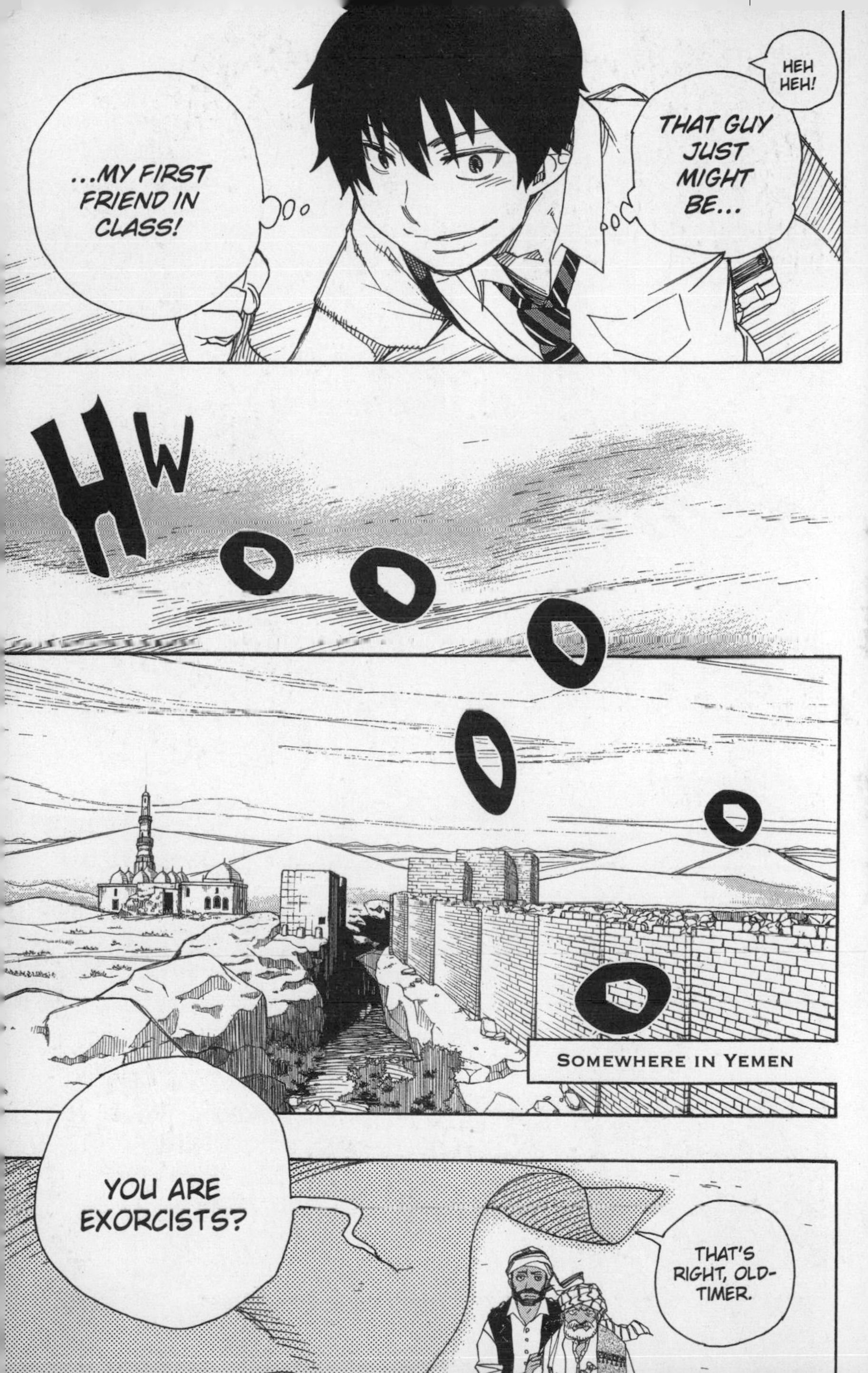
HEH HEH!
THAT GUY JUST MIGHT BE...
...MY FIRST FRIEND IN CLASS!
HWOOOOOO
SOMEWHERE IN YEMEN
THAT'S RIGHT, OLD-TIMER.
YOU ARE EXORCISTS?

PLEASE DO NOT FEAR.
TRMBL
KOFF KOFF HARDLY ANYONE CAN SEE THE MONSTERS...
TRMBL
...BUT I CAN! THEY'RE TO BLAME FOR EVERYTHING!
PEOPLE ARE DYING IN TOWN.
SPARKLE
SPARKLE
I, ARTHUR AUGUSTE ANGEL, WILL UTTERLY DESTROY THE DEMONS!

FWOO

THE *IMPURE PRINCESS* HAS RETURNED.

The impure princess wreaked havoc in the middle ages.
Whoa! That's huge!
She is a remnant of the impure clan.
She's a pet of Astaroth, King of Rot.
Her "heart" was split in two and sealed in the Yemen branch.

Yes, but an attacker stole those two hearts.
And then about five hours ago, an impure castle began forming and spewing poisonous gas.
According to a survivor of the attack...

...The attacker was a woman...
...who *ate* both of the hearts!

HMM
HMM
HMM
HMM
LIGHTNING...
HMM! I SENSE A CONNECTION.
OHHH? ♪ THAT SOUNDS A LOT LIKE THE IMPURE KING INCIDENT IN JAPAN.
HWOOO
...THEY SENT BOTH OF US HERE...
...BUT LEAVE THE IMPURE PRINCESS TO ME.
SERIOUSLY?
YOU'RE NOT WORRIED ABOUT MY SAFETY, ARE YOU?
NO, THAT'S NOT IT.
DID YOU HEAR WHO DEFEATED THE IMPURE KING?
UH-HUH.
You're not worried about me...

IT WAS SATAN'S CHILD!
WHEN THE IMPURE KING AWAKENED...
...AS PALADIN, I SHOULD HAVE BEEN THE ONE TO DESTROY HIM.
THEY DIDN'T EVEN TELL ME...
...AND THEY HAD THE SON OF SATAN DO IT INSTEAD!!
URGH
DADUM
I MUST SEIZE THIS OPPORTUNITY TO ASSERT MY STRENGTH AS PALADIN...
...AND SAVE THE PEOPLE FROM DEMONS!!
UH-HUH...
WHAT AN OVERLY STRONG SENSE OF DUTY!!
I STAND IN AWE!
I'D JUST SLOW YOU DOWN! FORGET ME AND GO!
THANK YOU, LIGHTNING!!
WORRY WORRY
TMP TMP TMP
GO, ANGEL, GOOOOO!!
SHOULD I TELL HIM THAT GUY'S BEING TOTALLY SARCASTIC?
SHH!
TOMP
CALIBURN! AWAKEN!

"LEND ME THY STRENGTH."
OOH ♡, ARTHUR!
BUT WHAT A STRONG OPPONENT!
TO DEFEAT THAT, I AT LEAST NEED SOME HAIR!
TUG
SHING
FWUP
YAAAY!
WOO-HOO! ♡
YOU GOT YOURSELF A DEAL!!
CRACKLE
CRACKLE

LET'S GO!
FWOO
ANGEL ...
SLASH !!!!

DM
DM
DM
DM
DM
DM
DM
THOOOM

DM
DM
DM
DM

BOOOMMM
RMMM
BOOSH
WHOA...
IN ONE STROKE!!
HE'S A *MONSTER!*

!
KRSH
IS THAT... THE WOMAN?!
LET'S GO, GUYS!
YES, SIR...

WOMAN...

FWISH

...WHO ARE YOU?

STOMP

GAH!

YEAH!

YOU HAG!

WHY DID YOU REVIVE THE IMPURE PRINCESS?

VEEN
AGH!
?!
BLUP
BLUP
WHSH
UGH
GAGAGH!
GYAAAH!!
AGH
BUT I...I...
I COULDN'T TOLERATE IT?!
...
YOU BASTARD ...
THE DAY IS COMING...
BLUP
BLUP
...WHEN ALL WILL BE ONE AND ALL EYES WILL SEE!!
BLUP
REMEMBER THIS...

POW
EXORCIIIIST!
WHAT JUST HAPPENED?
...
HWOOO

The Vatican

Underground: Knights of the True Cross Headquarters
You mean to say...

...That the woman swallowed the impure princess, thereby *voluntarily* falling to demonhood?

YES. AND HER BODY DISAPPEARED SOON AFTER.
SHE SAID SHE COULDN'T "TOLERATE" IT.
ACCORDING TO REPORTS ON THE IMPURE KING INCIDENT, SABUROTA TODO SWALLOWED KARURA.
THERE'S AN INTERNATIONAL WARRANT OUT FOR HIS ARREST.
WAS TODO ABLE TO "TOLERATE" IT?
I'D LIKE TO KNOW.
THE INCIDENTS INVOLVING TODO AND THIS WOMAN ARE SIMILAR.
THEY BOTH INGESTED A DEMON WITH A HIGH CAPACITY FOR CELL PROLIFERATION.

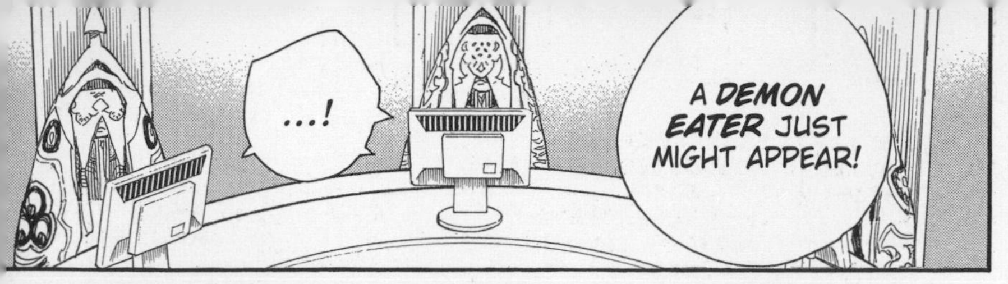

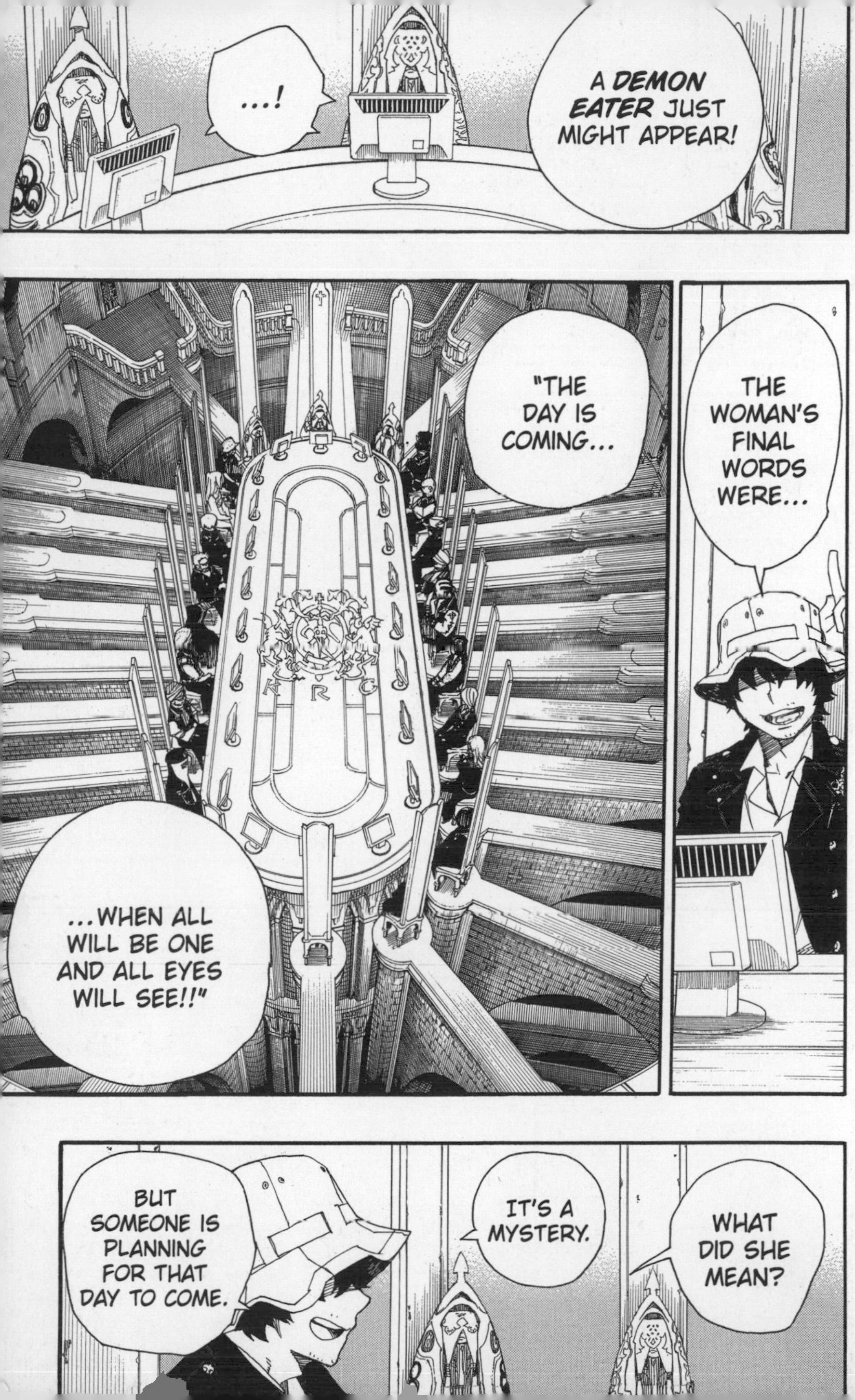

THE WOMAN'S FINAL WORDS WERE...

"THE DAY IS COMING...

...WHEN ALL WILL BE ONE AND ALL EYES WILL SEE!!"

INVESTIGATE ALL SUSPECT ORGANIZATIONS FROM DEMONIC CULTS TO ANTI-HUMAN ORGANIZATIONS AND SECRET SOCIETIES...

...AND REMAIN ALERT FOR DEMONS WHO FIT THE CONDITIONS THAT LIGHTNING MENTIONED.

UNDER-STOOD!

FWIP

UM, EXCUSE ME...

...BUT WHAT ABOUT...

...RIN OKUMURA?

...

...

...

WE SHALL DEFER HIS CASE UNTIL LATER.
OBSERVE HIM AND KEEP HIM UNDER CONTROL.
THE DEMON-EATER INVESTIGATION TAKES PRIORITY!

NICE DECISION!
AS YOU WISH! ☆

TCH!

FIND THE DEMON EATER!!

KACHAK
WELCOME BACK, MASTER.
CHAK
WELL DONE.
CONVEY THE CONTENTS OF THE MEETING TO ALL DEPARTMENTS.
AS YOU WISH.
WHEW...
FUMP
ASSIAH HAS ALWAYS LAIN...
...UNDER THREAT OF A DEMONIC INVADER FROM GEHENNA...

...WITH THE EXORCISTS FIGHTING ON THE BORDERLINE BETWEEN...

...BUT NOW THAT BORDER IS BLURRING.

WELL...

...NOW *THEY'RE* ON THE MOVE TOO.

POOF

CHATTER
CHATTER
MORNING, OKUMURA!
GOOD MORNING!
GOOD MORNING!!
I WANT TO ASK YOU GUYS SOMETHING.

OKUMURA !!
WHAT'S THAT?
IS TH-TH-THAT...
HUH?

...A *LOVE* LETTER?!
WHAT?!
HUH?!! WHY *YOU?!* NO FAIR!!
S-SERIOUSLY?
I'VE GOT A SECRET FAN!
BADUMP
BADUMP
I'M NOT SURPRISED.
To Rin Okumura
From Mephisto
LOVE
MORNIN', GUYS.
WHAZZAT?

GACK
IT'S FROM *MEPHISTO?!*
TOUGH BREAK, HUH?
PAT PAT
SHIMA! DON'T TOUCH ME!! I MEAN IT!!
HIS STATIONERY TOTALLY CREEPS ME OUT!!
FWACK
GYAH
DON'T FLAME UP, OKAY?
FATHER...
WHO, *ME?!*
Stop that!!
GYAAAH!!!
?!
GAH
GASP
OKUMURA ?!
CHATTER
CHATTER

GAH!

EEK!

WHOA!

AAAGH!

STAY AWAY!!

GODAIIN!

O...

OKU...

...MU...

...RA...

Blue Exorcist Chapter 38: Exorcist

IT'S FROM MEPHISTO ?!
HIS STATIONERY TOTALLY CREEPS ME OUT!!
FWAP
DESPITE THE WAY IT LOOKS, MAYBE IT'S IMPORTANT.
HURRY UP AND READ IT.
UGH. I DON'T WANNA...
BON, YOU'RE LIKE SOMEBODY'S FATHER!
WHO'S LIKE A FATHER, KONEKOMARU?!
S-SORRY...
HM? WHAT'S THIS MEAN?
LEMME SEE.
CHAPTER 39: DEMON MANNERS
FWIP
Rin Okumura,
The weather has been abnormally hot here at the beginning of autumn, but I hope you are doing well. I'm fine!
I have something to report!
Regarding your death sentence handed down by the Vatican the other day...it has been SUSPENDED!!!
Yaay! CLAP CLAP CLAP CLAP
You did it! Congratulations!!!

CHATTER
IT SAYS YOUR EXECUTION HAS BEEN SUSPENDED!!
EXECUTION?
I FORGOT ABOUT THAT!
I FIGURED IT WAS ABOUT YOUR SENTENCE.
BUT IT'S JUST SUSPENDED.
I DON'T LIKE IT.
CHATTER
HOW COULD YOU FORGET IT?!
I forgot too.
YOU'RE AMAZING, OKUMURA...
THERE'S ANOTHER PAGE.
By the way! If you're free this evening, let's celebrate the suspension of your sentence!!
Would you please come for evening cuisine at my mansion? Wear formal attire and come to the residence of Johann Faust on the top level of the academy by 6 PM.
I'll be waiting!
Mephisto
FLIP
Huh...?
WHAT'S THIS MEAN?
THE STATIONERY AND HAND-WRITING ARE SCARY!
I've got a bad feeling...
"C...CUI..." HOW DO YOU READ THIS?
CUISINE!!
THAT'S WHAT YOU DIDN'T GET?!
WHAT'S "CUISINE"?
YOU NEED TO STUDY!!
Google it!
GRAH!
Huh...?

FATHER...
It means supper.
WHO ME ?!
Stop that!
GYAAAAH!!
AIEE!
GAH!
AAAGH!
STAY AWAY!!
WHSH
THAT'S GODAIIN'S VOICE!!
OKUMURA!
GODAIIN!!
O...
OKU...
... MURA ...

WHEEZ
WHAT HAPPENED ?!
WHAT'S THAT?!
I'LL GET A TEACHER!
HUFF
HUFF
WHEEZ
WHEEZ
WHEEZ
WHEEZ
WHEEZ
WHEEZ
WHEEZ
UUU...
...AAAGH!!
HELP!!
...!!
DISAPPEAR...

?!

SWUF

SWF

SWF

SWF

SWF

SWF

SWF

DISAPPEAR!!!!

WHEEZ

GLURK

WHAT HAPPENED ?!

CHATTER

CHATTER

GODAIIN...

I CAN'T TAKE IT...

SOMEBODY HELP ME!!

Chapter 39: Demon Manners

Health Room
保健室
LISTEN...
...FREAKING OUT LIKE THAT JUST ATTRACTS THEM.
BUT...
...I'M WEAK!
MAYBE THAT'S WHY I CAN SEE THEM!
I WANNA BE NORMAL AGAIN!
CHAK
OKAY. JUST WAIT.
OKUMURA?
SWUF
...

LUNCHTIME

DO YOU GUYS KNOW A WAY TO STOP SEEING DEMONS?

I'VE NEVER HEARD OF ONE.

THEY SAY YOU CAN'T CUT THE BOND OF TEMPTAINT.

GODAIIN DOESN'T KNOW HOW HE GOT IT.

WHAT? THAT CAN HAPPEN?

Superb memory!

GODAIIN'S FATHER IS AN ASSEMBLYMAN, ISN'T HE?

ARE YOU GUYS FRIENDS?

Assemblyman?

NO, BUT I WANT TO BE.

HE SEEMS LIKE A NICE GUY.

OOH, LOOK! ♡

Like...

...Konekomaru.

Fanks.

IZUMO! PAKU!!

COME EAT WITH US!!

GEH!

WHAT A PEST !!

GRAH
GIMME A BREAK!!
I'M NOT SO DESPERATE THAT I'D EAT WITH *YOU* GUYS!!
IZUMO ...

THEN EVERYTHING'S NORMAL!!
PHEW!
THEY ALWAYS GO THROUGH THIS...
HE'S OPTIMISTIC TO THE POINT OF MASOCHISM!
HEY, IZUMO!!

DO YOU KNOW A WAY TO STOP SEEING DEMONS?
!!

OF...

OF COURSE NOT...
...YOU AWKWARD MIDDLE-SCHOOLER!
NOT SO LOUD!
OW!
THEY'LL JUST THINK WE'RE DISCUSSING A VIDEO GAME.

TCH! I'LL HAVE TO ASK YUKIO OR SHURA AT CRAM SCHOOL.
He isn't answering his phone.
OH, I FORGOT.
MNCH
MNCH

MR. OKUMURA SAID...
...THERE'S NO CRAM SCHOOL TODAY.
HUH?

YOU SAW YUKIO?
HE WAS AT MORNING CLASSES.
I'm in his class.
I HAVE TO TELL THE GIRLS TOO.
See ya.
ARGH! WHAT SHOULD I DO THEN?
RUSTLE
!
WHAT'S BEEN GOING ON SINCE YESTERDAY?
HAS THERE BEEN ANOTHER BIG INCIDENT?
UGH. DON'T SCARE ME, KONEKO!
AHA!
TAK
TAK
TAK

OKAY, BYE.
TAK
TAK
SHURA...
BIP
YUKIO!
TMP
TMP
ARE YOU GOING TO JOIN THE ANGELIC LEGION?
DON'T SAY THAT NAME!
IT'S SO EMBARRASSING I COULD DIE...
BLUSH
A MASSIVE NUMBER OF DEMONS ARE GATHERING AT A WASTE RESEARCH FACILITY.
IT COULD HAVE SOMETHING TO DO WITH...
...THE *DEMON EATER.*
YOU SEEM BUSY TOO.
THE ORDER HAS BEEN GETTING A LOT OF CONSULTATIONS.
I'VE GOT A BAD FEELING.
BE CAREFUL.
YOU, TOO.
TMP
TMP
OH, RIGHT...

...ARE YOU BLOWING OFF YOUR HEALTH CHECKUPS?

TMP

YEAH. I'M TOO BUSY.

YOU BETTER GO! The medics are complaining.

TMP

OKAY!

THIS IS PERFECT!

WELCOME, RIN OKUMURA!

KNIGHTS OF THE TRUE CROSS:
TOP LEVEL
JOHANN FAUST'S MANSION

MEPHISTO MIGHT KNOW A WAY TO STOP SEEING DEMONS!

FANK OOH FOH WAITING! ☆

BELIAL, I WILL PREPARE THE FOOD.

YOU MAY LEAVE US.

AS YOU WISH, MASTER.

ARE YOU...

...AN *OTAKU*?

YES!

INDEED I AM!!

I LOVE ALL ENTERTAINMENT FROM ASSIAH! ☆

BAM
ESPECIALLY JAPAN'S!!
JAPAN'S SORDID GREED FOR ENTERTAINMENT ISN'T MERELY AWE-INSPIRING—IT IS GOD-LIKE!
AND THESE DAYS, JAPAN HAS BECOME AN EASY PLACE FOR OTAKU TO LIVE!!
DA DUM
HUMAN IMAGINATION AND CREATIVITY CAN RIVAL THE EVIL POWERS OF DEMONS!
HMM
I BELIEVE WE WILL SOMEDAY HAVE THE TECHNOLOGY TO ENTER INTO VIDEO GAMES AND ANIME!
WHO ARE YOU TALKING TO?
WHO DO YOU THINK?
MWA HA HA
DON'T "MWA HA HA" ME!
I HAVE SOMETHING I WANNA TALK—
EINS!
ZWEI!
DREI!
SNAP
POOF
POF
WHOA!!

POOF
HAVE A SEAT, OKUMURA! ♪
LET'S EAT!
THIS IS *MATEKIYA*—MY FAVORITE INSTANT NOODLES! IT'S SPECIAL SUPER-SPICY PORK MISO RAMEN!
魔笛家
...
OH?
I THOUGHT I TOLD YOU TO DRESS FORMALLY!
YOUR MANNERS ARE AWFUL.
WHICH PARENT DO YOU TAKE AFTER?
BUT YOU'RE ONLY SERVING JUNK FOOD!
This whole thing is ridiculous!
WE'VE GOT FIVE MINUTES TO TALK UNTIL THE RAMEN IS READY.
RIGHT!
I NEED TO TALK TO YOU ABOUT SOMETHING!
?!
NO, I HAVE SOMETHING TO TALK TO *YOU* ABOUT.

YOU'VE FINALLY EARNED...
...THE RIGHT TO SPEAK TO ME.
HUH? WHAT AN ELITIST ATTITUDE!
WELL, I AM ELITE.
...ZWEI... EINS...
...DREI!
SNAP
DURING MY YEARS IN ASSIAH, I HAVE PICKED UP MANY NAMES.
!
"LOKI..."
...."TRICK-STER"...
...AND "WATARI GARASU," THE RAVEN.
I HAVE GONE BY "MEPHISTO PHELES" FOR 200 YEARS, BUT IT IS NOT MY ORIGINAL NAME.
GW

IN GEHENNA, I AM THE SECOND MOST POWERFUL BEING...
...AND KNOWN AS SAMAEL, KING OF TIME.
I AM ONE OF THE DEMON ROYALTY KNOWN AS THE BAAL.
WH...
WHAT?

YOU...
YOU'RE A *DEMON?!*
MWA HA HA! WHY SO SURPRISED?
IT'S AN OPEN SECRET!
YOU'RE THE ONLY ONE WHO DIDN'T KNOW.
WH-WHERE ARE WE?!
WHAT DID YOU DO?!
THIS IS GEHENNA.
...!!
URGH
WHY YOU...
I KNEW YOU WERE SKETCHY!
NOW YOU'VE REVEALED YOUR *TRUE NATURE!!!!*
BWOO
SH

CALM YOURSELF.
I HAVE CONTROL OVER SPACE AND TIME.
I HAVE SHIFTED OUR CONSCIOUSNESSES TO GEHENNA VIA DIMENSIONAL TRAVEL.
JUST GIVE ME FIVE MINUTES. ☆

...OUTTA HERE!!
SIGH
OH DEAR...
?!
!
I TOLD YOU... I CAN CONTROL SPACE AND TIME.

GYAAAH!
TUG
WHEN DID YOU-!!
A DEMON'S WEAKNESS IS HIS TAIL, AS WELL AS...
...HIS HEART.
I STOPPED TIME...
...SO I COULD BORROW IT. ☆
WHAH ?!
THIS SWORD HOLDS...
...YOUR DEMON HEART.

A DEMON'S VITAL SPOT IS HIS HEART.
ITS DESTRUCTION MEANS *DEATH.*
THE HEART IS ALSO A SOURCE OF STRENGTH.
WHEN EXPOSED LIKE THIS...
...YOU CAN DRAW UPON YOUR TRUE POWER...
...BUT YOU ALSO LEAVE YOUR VITAL POINT DEFENSELESS.
FOR THAT REASON, MOST DEMONS *HIDE* THEIR TAIL AND HEART.
So do I!!
THAT'S JUST *DEMON MANNERS...* ETIQUETTE, IF YOU WILL.
SEEING YOU WITH THEM *HANGING OUT* IS EMBARRASSING!
KCH
!

BUT INSTEAD OF EXPLAINING...
...HOW ABOUT A FIGHT?
SNAP
EINS!
ZWEI!
DREI!
LEARN JUST HOW UNSIGHTLY YOU ARE!

W
... RIN... O...
...KU..
...MURA.
!!
I KNOW THAT GUY!!
WHAT WAS HIS NAME...?
KLINK
Shoppai-man?
Suppai-mon?
YOU HAVEN'T BEATEN ME YET!
IF I USED MY TRUE POWER, I COULD EASILY...
TSK. GOING OVERBOARD WILL DESTROY YOUR HOST BODY.
THEN YOU COULDN'T STAY IN ASSIAH.
AND IT'S UNSEEMLY, SO CONTROL YOURSELF.
SHUT UP, BRO!!
OKEY-DOKEY! ♪

WHAM
FWUFF
GRAAAAAH!!!!
BWUMP
BWUMP
BWUMP
BWUMP
BWUMP
BWUMP
CRIK
CRAK
POP
KRAK
WOOSH
SHWUF

GRAAAAAH!
NOW WE'RE EQUAL!
GO
HUFF
HUFF
OM
I JUST REMEMBERED!

YOU'RE KARAIMON !!
BOOM
POW
NO, IT'S AMAIMON !!!!

WOOO
POOO
KRASH
I'VE NEVER FELT THIS WAY BEFORE!
I WON'T JUST MINCE YOU UP–I'LL GRIND YOU INTO BLOODY VOMIT!!
I WARNED YOU.
SIGH
HUH?
STAGGER
DRIP
SKIDD
BAM
WHAM

AMAIMON TARNISHES THE LOWEST SEAT OF THE BAAL.

HE IS KING OF EARTH, AND THE SEVENTH OF US.

ZSH ZSH

FSSHHHH

INCLUDING ME, THERE ARE SIX KINGS ABOVE HIM.

SNAP

SATAN STANDS EVEN HIGHER, RULING OVER ALL.

This is rated R. ★ We better censor it.

OH...

???
HEH HEH HEH! ☆

THESE EYEDROPS WILL REMOVE THE DEMON SIGHT.

AH!!
HOW DID YOU-
I SEE *MANY THINGS.*

GIVE IT HERE!!
Gimme!
HOW RUDE.
IT ISN'T *FREE,* YOU KNOW.

POOF
I'M ASSIGNING YOU HOMEWORK.
?!
Home-work?!
WHEN IT'S DONE, YOU MAY HAVE THIS.

EVIL FORCES HAVE BEGUN TO INFILTRATE ASSIAH.

HUH?

GODAIIN'S PROBLEM IS BUT A *HARBINGER* OF WHAT IS TO COME.

OOPSIE! FIVE MINUTES IS UP! ☆

POOF

DIG IN!!

WHUP

I'VE ALSO PREPARED RICE, SO NO WORRIES!

...

SOMEWHERE IN RUSSIA

HWOOOO

GYAH

THERE'S NO END TO THEM!

SYAAAH!
WHY ARE THERE SO MANY DEMONS HERE?!!
"ONLY THE RIGHTEOUS MAY LOOK UPON THE HOLY FACE"!!
GYAAH

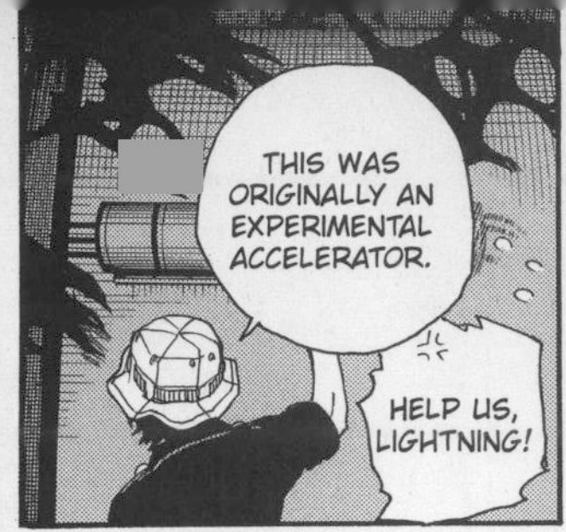
THIS WAS ORIGINALLY AN EXPERIMENTAL ACCELERATOR.
HELP US, LIGHTNING!

PERHAPS...
MUTTER MUTTER

TONK
HEY!

THERE'S SOMETHING FREAKY UP AHEAD.

FW
OOO

WHAT'S THIS?!
AH HA HA!!
?!
NICE...
THIS IS GETTING INTERESTING!
LIGHTNING, WHAT'S GOING ON?!
I BET THIS IS...
...A GATE TO GEHENNA!

Blue Exorcist Chapter 39: Demon Manners

Chapter 40: The Seven Mysteries of True Cross Academy

A GEHENNA GATE?!

I THOUGHT ONLY SATAN COULD MAKE THOSE!

DOES THAT MEAN SATAN WAS HERE?!

IMPOSSIBLE !!
HEY...
...IS THAT THING EXPANDING?!
V
M
THE LITTLE DEMONS ARE PROLIFERATING TOO!
STAYING HERE COULD BE DANGEROUS, ANGEL.
M
M
M
SKRAA!
GEH HEH!
M
CAN'T WE BLOCK THE GATE?
WELL, *WE* CERTAINLY CAN'T.
WE NEED A SPECIALIST.
HA HA HA!!
AH HA HA!
M
!!

YOU MEAN ***MEPHISTO?***

YOU MAY NOT WANT HIS HELP...

...BUT WE-

I KNOW!!

ANGELIC LEGION! FALL BACK!!!

BUT NOW I HAVE AN IDEA WHO WE'RE UP AGAINST!
CHATTER
CHATTER
CHATTER
KNIGHTS OF THE TRUE CROSS: JAPAN BRANCH CONSULTATION CENTER
I'VE BEEN SEEING A BLACK GOO...
...CREEP OUT OF THE KITCHEN SINK!
EVERY NIGHT!
BY MY BED!!
I'M CURSED !!

FIRST, CLEAN OUT THE DRAIN.
Like with bleach.
THEN POUR IN THIS HOLY WATER, WAIT FIVE MINUTES, AND RINSE IT OUT.
HOLYWATER
OKAY.

IT'LL BE FINE.
SMILE
IF YOU STILL SEE IT, COME VISIT ME AGAIN.

THERE USED TO BE DAYS WHEN NOT A SINGLE PERSON CAME IN. I WONDER WHAT'S BEEN GOING ON RECENTLY?
What a handsome young man!

I NEED TO GO TO THE MEDICS FOR A CHECKUP TODAY...
BVVT
BVVT

PI
THIS IS OKUMURA.
MR. OKUMURA, YOU SOUND BUSY.
CHATTER
CHATTER
LORD PHELES...
WHAT IS IT?

Chapter 40: The Seven Mysteries of True Cross Academy

OKAY...
...IT'S BEEN THREE DAYS.
AFTER THAT TIME OFF, I'M SORRY TO CALL YOU HERE AT THIS HOUR.

11:00 PM
WE'RE GOING TO HAVE A SPECIAL LESSON.
SPECIAL?

IT INVOLVES A MISSION DIRECTLY FROM LORD PHELES.
FOLLOW ME.
YAWN
OKAY...
RIN, YOUR HAIR'S DIFFERENT TODAY.
HUH?
YEAH. I HAD DINNER WITH MEPHISTO LAST NIGHT...
RUB
RUB

YOU WENT?!
HOW WAS IT?
WELL, UH...
HOW IS IT??
SCRUMPTIOUS, RIGHT?!
IT'S DELICIOUS! SPICY AND DELICIOUS!
TING -A- LING!
DING -A- DING!
*ANIME SONG
HELLO?
THIS IS MEPHISTO PHELES! ☆
BIP
Delicious! This has pepper in it!
SLURRRP
...
I'LL BE THERE RIGHT AWAY.
SOMETHING HAS COME UP.
MMM?
CHAK
SO WHAT'S MY HOMEWORK?
I'LL HAVE YOUR BROTHER ASSIGN IT.
GASP
HUH? YUKIO?
MR. OKUMURA...

I'M GLAD YOUR EXECUTION WAS SUSPENDED...

...BUT IT'S JUST A *SUSPENSION.*

WHILE THIS REPRIEVE LASTS...

...

...GET YOUR ACT TOGETHER AS A DEMON.

I WILL MAKE EVERY EFFORT TO COOPERATE.

IS HE ACTUALLY A DECENT GUY?

HMM... WELL...

I HAD SOME AWESOME, SPICY INSTANT RAMEN.

INSTANT NOODLES ?!

MEPHISTO WAS JUST MESSING WITH YOU...

IT'S AROUND HERE.

ALL RIGHT, LISTEN UP.

YOU KNOW HOW EVERYONE HAS BEEN TALKING ABOUT THE *SEVEN SCHOOL MYSTERIES*, RIGHT?

!
THE SEVEN MYSTERIES!! GODAIIN MENTIONED THOSE!

THE GIRLS HAVE BEEN EXCITED ABOUT THEM!
THEY'RE A BIG TOPIC RECENTLY.

I'M GOING TO HAVE YOU TAKE ON...
...THE DEMONS BEHIND THOSE RUMORS.

HUH ?!
ALL BY OURSELVES ?
YES.
MEPHISTO! SO THIS WAS HIS "HOMEWORK"!
I WILL OBSERVE, BUT I WILL NOT INTERVENE...
...IN YOUR STRATEGY OR THE ACTUAL FIGHTING.
THE PRECEPTOR WANTS YOU TO WORK TOGETHER.
I'LL HAND OUT A LIST OF THE MYSTERIES.
THE SEVEN MYSTERIES OF TRUE CROSS ACADEMY
1. A FORM DRESSED IN WHITE THAT WANDERS THE ACADEMY AT NIGHT.
2. A STATUE OF JOHANN FAUST AT MEPPHYLAND THAT STARTS MOVING AT NIGHT.
3. TOILET MAYUKO IN THE GIRLS' DORMITORY.
4. A PICTURE OF YOURSELF DEAD THAT APPEARS BETWEEN THE PORTRAITS IN THE HIGH SCHOOL.
5. AN EMPTY STREETCAR THAT TRAVELS THE STREETS AT NIGHT.
6. A WUNDERKAMMER THAT APPEARS IN THE HIGH SCHOOL CHEMISTRY LAB.
7. A MANSION YOU CAN NEVER REACH.
THESE ARE THE SEVEN MYSTERIES THAT EVERYONE HAS BEEN TALKING ABOUT.

TAP
THE FIRST ONE YOU ARE GOING UP AGAINST...
...IS THE WHITE APPARITION THAT WANDERS THE ACADEMY AT NIGHT!
ACCORDING TO THE INFORMATION WE HAVE...
...IT'S THE GHOST OF A BRIDE.
SHE ATTACKS MEN WHO NOTICE HER AT NIGHT...
...BUT WON'T APPEAR AROUND WOMEN.
SHE HAS BEEN INVOLVED IN TWELVE INCIDENTS IN TWO WEEKS.
!!
THERE!

A WHITE SHAPE!!

THERE SHE IS.

BEGIN THE MISSION.

That was fast!!

HUH?!

ALREADY?!

DON'T FORGET ABOUT *TEAMWORK.*

NOW GET TO IT!

ARIAS ARE THE BEST FOR EXPELLING A GHOST.
A WHITE-ROBED BRIDE COULD BE EITHER BUDDHIST OR SHINTO...
SHOULD WE USE A SHINTO PRAYER OR A SUTRA?

NEKO AND SHIMA AND I WANT TO BE ARIAS...
...SO WE'LL CHANT ALL KINDS OF PRAYERS AND SUTRAS.
Oh...
HUH ?!
...

ALL RIGHT, THEN...
...I'LL DISTRACT THE WHITE FIGURE...
...TO GIVE YOU MORE TIME!!
!
SOUNDS GOOD.

TAKARA, YOU WANT TO BE A TAMER...
...SO WHAT KIND OF FAMILIAR HAVE YOU GOT?
...

BABAM
SHUT UP! DON'T TALK TO ME!
JUST DO WHAT YOU WANT!
GAMP
GAMP

HA HA HA...

RRRM

MMMM

BON!!

CONTROL YOURSELF!

LEAVE TAKARA HERE THEN!

LET'S GO!

DADUN

YEAH!

WORRY

WORRY

WE HAVEN'T DONE THIS FOR A WHILE!

YOU'RE AWFULLY RELAXED, SHIMA!

IN A PINCH, OKUMURA CAN JUST ROAST IT WITH HIS BLUE FLAME! ♪

SHH! CONCENTRATE!

EVENING, MISS!
OH MY...
...WHAT A CUTE BOY!! ♡♡♡
YOU CAN SEE ME?

PWUMP
HM ...?
YOU'RE A CROSS-DRESSER?!
THAT WAS DIRECT!!!!
HOW COULD YOU SAY THAT?!
IT'S NOT THAT SIMPLE!!
BUMMP
?!
OW!
SWOO
IN LIFE...
...I HAD TO HIDE MY FEMININE HEART!
I WANTED TO PLAY WITH DOLLS AND WEAR GIRLS' CLOTHING...
...BUT I HAD TO PRETEND I WAS A BOY!
THEN I DIED.
BUT...
!

URRGH
I WAS FINALLY SUPPOSED TO BE MY TRUE SELF...
...SINCE I WAS DISHONEST WITH MYSELF, I COULDN'T PASS ON!!
GAAAH
...BUT YOU CALL ME A CROSS-DRESSER?!
BUT AREN'T YOU?
ANYWAY, JUST GIMME A KISS! ♡♡♡
GRAB
?!
Hmm...
SORRY, BUT...
I NEVER KISS CROSS-DRESSING DEAD PEOPLE ON THE FIRST DATE.

COULDN'T HE BE A LITTLE GENTLER?!
A DIRECT REFUSAL!!!!
WE SHOULD HAVE HAD SHIMA DO THAT.
Sorry!
NO WAY, KONEKO!!
DON'T BE SO MEAN!!
HMFF!
TRMBL
TRMBL
TRMBL
I DO LIKE HONEST BOYS, THOUGH!
BUT...
...UNTIL I FIND MY SOULMATE...
RRRRRIP
GASP
...I'LL NEVER STOP LOOKING!!
OOH MY! ♡♡♡
GAH!
MORE YOUNG CUTIES!!

WHOOSH
HERE I COME, BOYS!!!!
PUCKER UP!!!!
DUT DUT DUT DUT DUT DUT DUT
W-WAIT!
SHIMA! PRAY TO AMIDA BUDDHA!
That's an easy one...
HUH?!
NEKO! THE LOTUS SUTRA!
I'LL START WITH THE SHINTO PRAYER, THEN JOIN YOU!!
UH... ...OKAY!!

OKUMURA!!
CLAP
NAMU AMIDA BUTSU ...
...NAMU AMIDA BUTSU!
MYOUHOU RENGE...
LEAVE THIS...
...TO ME!!
FWOOSH
KNOCK IT OFF, YOU!!
CLOMP
EEEEEK!

HUH?!
GHOSTS ARE COMPOSED OF GAS-LIKE PARTICLES.
THEY CAN DISSIPATE AND REFORM AT WILL.
PHYSICAL ATTACKS WON'T WORK.
FWSH
?!
WHY DID YOU DO THAT? I HATE YOU!
Uh-oh...
SERIOUSLY ?!
FIRE IS EFFECTIVE, BUT WHEN A GHOST DISSIPATES, THERE'S NOTHING TO BURN.

ONE KISS AND I'LL KNOW IF YOU'RE THE ONE!!
OM
MP
SMOOTCHIE, SMOOTCHIE!!
TRMBL
NA...
NAMU AMU...
"A"
TRMBL
TRMBL
TRMBL
...
UH-OH. I MESSED UP...
HOW CAN YOU MESS THAT ONE UP?!
JIGAKYUU SEIZOU...
HEH
BON! KONEKO! SORRY!!
SHIMA?!
OOKAMI NO TAME NI...
IHOU BENRIKIKO...
SH
SHIMA ?!
WH
SHIMA! I'M SPEECHLESS!!
H
SHUJOU SHOYUURAKU...
MICHIBIKI SAZUKE-TAMAE...
I WON'T FORGET THIS, SHIMA!!
GAAAA

TADUM
OH MY! SO CUTE!
I ABSOLUTELY LOVE MONKS! ♡
!!
UMAN-DARAGE...
...SANBUTSU KYOUDAIJU...
LEAVE THEM ALONE!!
EEK!
SWSH
URGH.
WHAT A PERSISTENT BOY!
FWSH
ARE YOU *JEALOUS?*
FWSH
SWSH
ARRRGH!
SWSH
WE AREN'T COMPATIBLE !!
HE'S SO POWERFUL...
..BUT DEPENDING ON THE OPPONENT, THINGS CAN END UP LIKE THIS.
B...
BUT HE *IS* BUYING TIME!

HARASOU GYATI...
...BOUJI SOUKA...
...
SILENCE
B...
BON!
I'M ALL OUT OF PRAYERS AND SUTRAS!
WHAT ELSE CAN WE TRY?!
...

IT'S NO USE! I CAN'T STOP HIM!!
WAAAH
RUN!!
UM, BON...?
H-HE SAID RUN!
BON!
KONEKO-MARU!
IT WON'T GO AWAY UNTIL IT KISSES A BOY!!
!!
WE SHOULD FALL BACK AND COME UP WITH A PLAN!
KISSY-KISSY MISSILE!!
SMACK
WHOA!
IT NEEDS...
...A KISS?
ULP

RR
YOU WON'T GET AWAY, BOYS!!
GYAAAH!!!
MMMM
GOTCHA! ♡
THWHAAMM
GAH!
OKAY, LET'S SMOOCH! ♡
NUH-UH, NUH-UH, NUH-UH! Y-YOU'RE FREAKING ME OUT!
GRAB
SHIMA!!
FOR GOD'S SAKE, NOOO!

WAAAAAH
THEIR FORMATION HAS CRUMBLED.
THEY'RE IN A PANIC.
MAYBE I SHOULD-
SIGH
TCH!
USELESS BRATS!
!

TOMP
!
OOH!
ANOTHER ONE!!
KISSY-KISSY MISSILE!!
GWSH
"COME FORTH!"
GAWP
"FASHION DOLL: MIKA'S FRIEND SERIES"!
"JEAN: BRIDEGROOM VERSION"!!!
POOF

SPARKLE
SPARKLE
MY DEAR BRIDE!
LET'S GET MARRIED!
SPARKLE
BABUMP
I FORGOT...
...THAT WHAT I REALLY ADMIRED WAS GIRLS.
I WANTED TO PLAY DOLLS AND WEAR GIRLS' CLOTHING...
OH, I SEE...
IT WASN'T KISSES THAT HE NEEDED!
GASP
!!

THANK YOU, BOYS...
NOW I HAVE NO REGRETS...
FWSH
I AM THE PUPPET MASTER!
I CAN SUMMON AND CONTROL PUPPETS!
HEH HEH HEH HEH
I DON'T HAVE A MEISTER, BUT I'M BETTER THAN YOU LOSERS!
CRAM SCHOOL'S BORING!
GAWP
JUST LEAVE ME ALONE!
GAWP

OH, SO *THAT'S* HOW IT IS, HUH?!
I'VE HAD ENOUGH OF THIS...
TRMBL TRMBL
TRMBL
CRIK
CRIK
CRIK
THEN JUST *QUIT* CRAM SCHOOL!!
DGAAH
KONEKO-MARU?
WHAT'S WITH YOU ?!
WHOA
STOP HIM, SHIMA!!
OH, HE'S STILL OUT FROM THAT KISS?
OKUMURA!! OKUMURA?!
OH, HE'S WIPED OUT TOO?
WAAAAH
WHAT'RE THOSE GUYS DOING?
EVERY-ONE!!

QUIET DOWN.
DO YOU WANT TO DIE?

NO...
Shut up!

KACHAK
KREEEAK
THE HONORABLE KNIGHT AND PRECEPTOR OF THE JAPAN BRANCH...
...LORD MEPHISTO PHELES!!

HMM...
IT SMELLS LIKE GEHENNA HERE...
CHATTER
CHATTER
THAT'S MEPHISTO PHELES?!
I'VE NEVER SEEN HIM BEFORE!
!!
HM?
HE GOT SHY!
OH DEAR, WHAT A MESS!
I DID NOT!!
Can't take a joke?
YOU NEVER CHANGE, ANGEL.
I'M SORRY YOU CALLED ME HERE...
...BUT EVEN I CAN'T CLOSE A GEHENNA GATE.
WHAT?!

THE GATE WILL CONTINUE TO WIDEN...
LOOK AT THIS.
...AND SLOWLY BUT SURELY...
ACCORDING TO TODAY'S KNIGHTS OF THE TRUE CROSS WEB NEWS...
...BRANCHES ALL OVER THE WORLD ARE EXPERIENCING INCREASED LEVELS OF ACTIVITY.
WHAT'S GOING ON?
...DEVOUR ASSIAH!

BLUE EXORCIST CHAPTER 40: THE SEVEN MYSTERIES OF TRUE CROSS ACADEMY

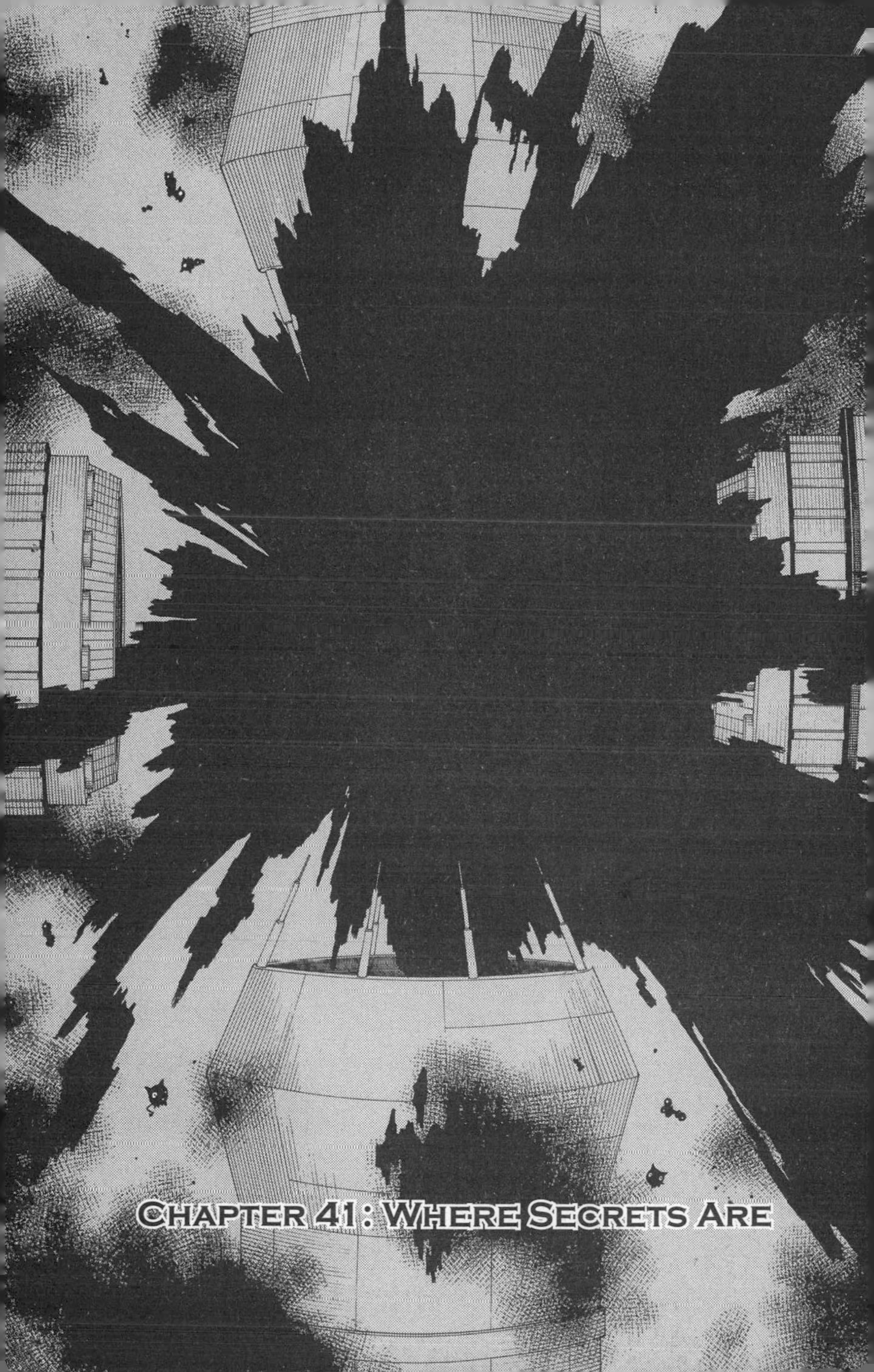
Chapter 41: Where Secrets Are

AT LEAST REPLY TO YOUR EMAILS!
SZZZZZZ
I NEED TO KNOW IF YOU NEED DINNER OR A BENTO!
SZZ
SZZ
SORRY, MOM.
SWIK
SWIK
WELL, YOUR MOM'S BEEN *WORRIED!!*
I'VE BEEN ROTATING BETWEEN THE CONSULTATION CENTER AND MISSIONS.
THE NUMBER OF CONSULTATIONS HAS BEEN ABNORMALLY HIGH.
I WAS REALLY BUSY.
I'D LIKE A MOM TOO, YOU JERK!
DOES THAT...
...HAVE SOMETHING TO DO WITH THE SUDDEN INTEREST IN THE SEVEN SCHOOL MYSTERIES?

IN OTHER WORDS, THERE ARE MORE PEOPLE LIKE GODAIIN.

PROBABLY. WE'RE STILL INVESTIGATING.

PUFF PUFF

WILL I BE DONE WITH MEPHISTO'S HOMEWORK IF WE SOLVE ALL SEVEN MYSTERIES?

THAT'S WHAT I HEARD.

SHUMP-
I HAVE TO TO FOCUS ON TEACHING AT THE CRAM SCHOOL.
IT'S KEEPING ME BUSY.
AND I HAVE SOMETHING ELSE TO DO FIRST.
UM...
...ARE YOU HIDING SOMETHING?
HUH?
WHY DO YOU ASK?
Huh?
WHY? I CAN'T SAY EXACTLY, BUT...
...YOU *SMILE* WHEN YOU'RE HIDING SOMETHING!
YOU'VE ALWAYS BEEN THAT WAY!
I'M NOT HIDING ANYTHING.
GOOD-BYE.

TAK TAK TAK
KACHAK CHAK
...
CLINK
CLINK
YUKIO'S HIDING SOMETHING.
I CAN SMELL IT!
KLATTR
TCH!
BUT HE WON'T TELL ME?!
TMP
TMP
OH, RIN!!
GOOD MORNING!
PEEK
OH!
SHIEMI? GOOD MORNING!

WHAT GIVES? YOU GUYS HAVE ME WORRIED...
HEH HEH HEH! BYE NOW!
GOOD LUCK WITH TODAY'S MISSION!
SKRF
THANKS! I'LL DO MY BEST!!
YOU TOO!
"YOU TOO"? HEH HEH!
SHIEMI'S AWFULLY CONFIDENT TODAY!
Why's she so peppy?
BUT.
SHE'S RIGHT, THOUGH.
UGH

ING DONG
DING DONG
DING DONG
CHATTER
I COULDN'T TAKE DOWN A SINGLE GHOST...
MR. OKUMURA SAID WE SHOULD REFLECT ON OUR FAILINGS...
...AND IDENTIFY SOLUTIONS FOR THE FUTURE.
CHATTER
I CAN'T. I ERASED ALL MEMORY OF YESTERDAY.
CHATTER
OW!
YOU NEED TO REFLECT MORE THAN ANYONE!!!
KICK
I WONDER WHO TAKARA REALLY IS...
HIS NAME IS *NEMU TAKARA.*
HE'S THE SON OF THE PRESIDENT OF THE TAKARA HOBBY TOY COMPANY.
HE'S A SECOND-YEAR, SO HE'S ONE YEAR OLDER THAN US.
HUH ?!!!

HE'S AN UPPER-CLASSMAN?! TAKARA HOBBY IS A HUGE COMPANY!
HE'S OLDER THAN US?!
IS THAT WHY HE'S SO ARROGANT ?!
SERIOUSLY?!
HE TRANSFERRED IN THIS YEAR.
THAT'S ALL I KNOW.
NOW HE'S EVEN MORE SHROUDED IN MYSTERY.
!!
WHAT'S THE MATTER, KONEKOMARU?
NOT FEELING WELL?
YOU DID WELL, SO THERE'S NOTHING TO WORRY ABOUT.

I'M F-FINE.
DON'T WORRY ABOUT ME.
REALLY?
I J-JUST WONDER...
...IF MORIYAMA AND KAMIKI WILL BE ALL RIGHT TODAY.

SILENCE
...
GOOD WORK, EVERYONE.

THE SEVEN MYSTERIES OF TRUE CROSS ACADEMY
1. A FIGURE DRESSED IN WHITE THAT WANDERS THE ACADEMY AT NIGHT.
2. A STATUE OF JOHANN FAUST AT MEPPHYLAND THAT STARTS MOVING AT NIGHT.
3. TOILET MAYUKO IN THE GIRL'S DORMITORY.
4. A PICTURE OF YOURSELF DEAD THAT APPEARS BETWEEN THE PORTRAITS IN THE HIGH SCHOOL.
5. AN EMPTY STREETCAR THAT TRAVELS THE STREETS AT NIGHT.
6. A WUNDERKAMMER THAT APPEARS IN THE HIGH SCHOOL CHEMISTRY LAB.
7. A MANSION YOU CAN NEVER REACH.
TOMORROW YOU WILL TAKE ON NUMBER THREE: *TOILET MAYUKO IN THE GIRLS' DORMITORY.*
THE NIGHT BEFORE
MS. KAMIKI, YOU LIVE IN THE DORM, SO YOU KNOW ABOUT THIS, RIGHT?
YES. IT'S A RUMOR ABOUT THE NORTH RESTROOM ON THE SIXTH FLOOR.
TELL US ABOUT IT.
ACCORDING TO THE RUMOR...
...SOME THIRD-YEAR STUDENTS TOOK A DARE RECENTLY AND GOT TRAPPED INSIDE.
WHEN THEY WERE FINALLY RESCUED, IT WAS LIKE THEIR SOULS WERE MISSING.
NOW THEY'RE ALL ABSENT FROM SCHOOL.
TOILET
NO ONE HAS GONE NEAR THAT RESTROOM EVER SINCE.
THAT STORY IS *TRUE.*
MAYUKO MAY BE AN EVIL GHOST.
UNLIKE THE WHITE FIGURE, SHE'S BAD BUSINESS, SO NO FOOLING AROUND.

ALSO UNLIKE THE WHITE FIGURE, MAYUKO ONLY APPEARS BEFORE *GIRLS.*

HUH? SO DOES THAT MEAN...

MS. KAMIKI AND MS. MORIYAMA MUST HANDLE THIS.

YES.

O-OKAY!!

L...

LET'S DO OUR BEST, KAMIKI!

DO "OUR" BEST?

YOUR FOCUS IS DEFENSE AND HEALING!

I'M THE ONE WHO'LL HAVE TO FIGHT!

WHY WOULD I NEED YOU TO–
MS. KAMIKI!
AT LEAST SHIEMI LEARNED SOMETHING FROM WATCHING THE BOYS' SHODDY PERFORMANCE!
SO COOPERATE!
SIGH
IZUMO!
LET'S GO GET SOME STATIONERY!
I'm outta notebooks!
PAKU!
EEK!
WHAT SHOULD I DO?!
?!

I NOTICED YOU'VE BEEN ON EDGE SINCE SUMMER BREAK.
AH...!
...DOESN'T MATTER!!
I CAN'T BELIEVE SHE HELPED ME!!
I DON'T WANT TO SAY IT!!
BUT IF I DON'T, I'LL FEEL BAD!
THEN JUST TELL HER.
WHY DON'T YOU LIKE MORIYAMA?
SHE'D NEVER DO ANYTHING TO HURT YOU.
THERE ISN'T ANY *REASON*!
I JUST DON'T WANT TO GET CLOSE TO ANYONE BUT YOU!!

PAKU, YOU KNOW...

...I HAVE A *REASON* TO BE HERE.

TRUE CROSS ACADEMY HIGH SCHOOL: NEW GIRLS DORMITORY

WE'RE NOT SNEAKING IN AT NIGHT? TOO BAD...

SHIMA ...

WE HAVE TO SETTLE THIS DURING THE DAY WHILE EVERYONE IS GONE.

FWOOOSH
I HUMBLY BESEECH THE GOD INARI...
...TO AID ME IN MY TIME OF NEED!!
BOOO BOOO
HEY! TODAY WAS THE RICE-HARVESTING FESTIVAL!
WE WERE EATING THE OFFERINGS!
You suck!
Get a clue!
SHUT UP AND COME WITH ME!

HERE IT IS.

KACHAK

CREEAK

WHOA...

WE'LL BE...
SWIP
...ON STANDBY HERE...
...SO GIVE IT ALL YOU'VE GOT.
UNDERSTOOD.
LET'S CHECK OUT THE STALLS.

THIS IS MY CHANCE.
I HAVEN'T BEEN PAIRED WITH HER SINCE KYOTO.

I NEED TO PAY HER BACK FOR SAVING ME!!
KAMIKI!

ONLY THIS ONE IS CLOSED!
...
PARDON ME!
IS SOMEONE IN THERE?
NOK NOK
NO, WAI-
YES...
I TOTALLY HATE YOU!
DON'T PLAY INNOCENT WITH ME!
YOU WON'T GET AWAY WITH IT JUST 'CAUSE YOU'RE CUTE!
HUH?
TCH!
JUST...

...GET ON WITH IT ALREADY!!

FWAM

W
...A CONCENTRATION OF GIRLS' SPITE.
SHE TOTALLY PISSES ME OFF! GRR!
HEE
TEE HEE!
HEE HEE HEE
HOW BORING! THAT SUCKS!
I WISH I HAD HER LOOKS!

HUH? FORMAL? THAT'LL TAKE SPIRIT POWER.
IT'S TIRING.
YAWN
?!
WE DON'T HAVE TO DO *THAT* MUCH FOR YOU!
DON'T THINK WE'LL *ALWAYS* OBEY YOU!!
WH...
WHAT?
AT LEAST GIVE US A LITTLE TREAT!
J-JUST DO WHAT I SAY!!
NO.
!!
SWSH
SWSH
SWSH
GRRRRR...
KAMIKI !!
SHWIP
SH
WMP
UNGH!

EEK!
WHAP
NEE!!
P... P... PWIF
SNAP
PWIF
PWIF
PWIF

FWIP FWIP FWIP
THANKS, NEE!
KOFF
KOFF
KAMIKI!
PANG
THE INARI AREN'T VERY COOPERATIVE...
GASP
I'VE GOT AN IDEA!
NEE!! GET ME SOME *URUCHI* AND *MOCHI* RICE PLANTS!!
NEE!!

NEEOOGH!!
FWUF
MMF!
FWUF
FWUF
SHUF
!
SHUMP
G-GREAT INARI GODS!
I CAN ONLY OFFER THESE RICE PLANTS...
...BUT PLEASE LEND US YOUR STRENGTH!!

YOU LIKE RICE, RIGHT?

BLUSH

...

ULP ?!

SHWIP

EEEEEEK!!

DRAG

GIRL!!

GRRRRR...

TEE HEE HEE! THOSE GODS ARE TOTALLY UNCOOL!

GRB

GRRRRIP
TEE HEE HEE! YOU'RE TRYING TO LOOK FASHIONABLE...
AGH!!
...BUT IT LOOKS AWFUL ON YOU! GRR! HOW PITIFUL! GRR!
GRRRRRRIP
UNNN...
PP
...!
KOFF
GRR
RP
BWSH
NEE NEE!!
!!
MORIYAMA!!
GRAB
SHIEMI!
WAIT!!
I GUESS THERE'S NO CHOICE...
TMP

WE'LL HELP FOR THAT GIRL'S SAKE.
HURRY UP AND CHANT A PRAYER!!
...!!
URGH...
CLAP
FURUE YURA YURA FURUE YURA YURA TO FURUE...
CLAP
...HIFUMI YOINAMUNAYA KOTOMOCHIRORANE ...
HOW DID THIS HAPPEN?! I WAS SUPPOSED TO PAY HER BACK!
CLAP
CLAP
...SHIKIRU YUITSUWANU SOWOTAHAKUMEKA ...
KAMI... KI...
TEE HEE HEE! GRRR!
I FEEL SORRY FOR YOU, SO I SHOULD TELL YOU...

...THAT SHE DOESN'T THINK OF YOU AS A FRIEND.
TOO BAD, SO SAD!
GRR! TEE HEE HEE!
THAT'S HILARIOUS!
TEE HEE HEE!
YOU THOUGHT SHE WAS YOUR FRIEND? HOW SAD...
...
I DON'T EVEN KNOW YOU...
...SO HOW WOULD YOU EVEN KNOW?!
GET LOST!

CLAP
...FURUE YURA YURA FURUE YURA YURA TO FURUE...
...MOMOCHI-YOROZU...
EXPEL SPIRIT!!!!

THANK YOU, KAMIKI!

...!!
I'LL NEVER SAY THIS AGAIN, SO LISTEN UP.
THANK YOU.
SHIEMI!! IZUMO!
CLAP
CLAP
CLAP
CLAP
NO PROBLEM!

TA DAH
WOW! THAT WAS AWESOME!!
CLAP
CLAP
YOU BOTH DID WELL!
CLAP
GREAT TEAMWORK!
CLAP
BFF FFT

AH HA HA HA HA!!
BUT...
WAH
HAH HAH HAH
AREN'T I KINDA CUTE?
KOFF
THAT'S "GETTING READY"?!
HA HA HA!!
HUH?! THAT'S SO TIGHT ON YOU!

THERE WASN'T AN EVIL GHOST LOOSE IN THE GIRLS' DORM BEFORE.
BUT IT GOT STRONG ENOUGH TO BECOME ONE OF THE SEVEN SCHOOL MYSTERIES.
GYA HA HA-HAKK KOFF
IT'S NOT *THAT* FUNNY, KAMIKI!

FWAP
...SECHS...
...FÜNF...
...VIER...
...DREI...
HWOOO
...ZWEI...
...EINS...
NULL.

SNAP
VERWEILE DOCH!
(STAY AWHILE)
TUNK

WHEW!!
I PUT A BARRIER AROUND THE GATE AND STOPPED TIME INSIDE.
FWI
SH
THAT WILL SLOW THE GATE'S EXPANSION.
BUT I CAN'T STOP TIME INDEFINITELY.
HOW LONG WILL IT LAST?
ABOUT FOUR TO FIVE MONTHS.
...!!
THE INCREASING NUMBER OF INCIDENTS WORLDWIDE...
...IS DUE TO GEHENNA'S INFLUENCE COMING THROUGH THE GATE.
IF IT OPENS ANY *WIDER*, UNIMAGINABLE *CALAMITY* AWAITS.

THERE'S ONLY ***ONE*** ORGANIZATION THAT HAS THE TECHNOLOGICAL AND FINANCIAL RESOURCES FOR SOMETHING LIKE THIS.

YOU KNOW THAT, RIGHT?

WHAT ARE YOU GETTING AT, LIGHTNING?

THE ILLUMINATI.

TAK
TAK
HOW ARE YOU FEELING, LEADER?
PSHHT
TODAY...
...I FEEL GREAT...
...TODO.
PSHHT
I CAME TO CONGRATULATE YOU...
...ON OPENING THE GEHENNA GATE.
THANK YOU.
PSHHT
PSHHT

BLUE EXORCIST 10
- END -

Blue Exorcist Chapter 41: Where Secrets Are

NO BUGS LIFE
Bonus Chapter: Kinzo's Band Doesn't Care

KAW
KAW
虎屋
TORAYA INN, KYOTO -AFTER THE BATTLE AGAINST THE IMPURE KING AND SIGHTSEEING IN KYOTO-
ARGH!
WE FINALLY GO BACK TO TOKYO TOMORROW...
...BUT WE'RE STILL SLAVING AWAY AT CHORES!
I'm dripping sweat everywhere I've wiped!
PLIP
PLIP
PLIP
I CAN'T STAND THIS HEAT...
FWAP
OH!
IZUMO!
SHE'S ALWAYS FROWNING...
YOU SHOULD SMILE SOMETIMES...
PAT
PAT

DO YOU *LIKE* THAT GIRL OR SOMETHING?
POKE POKE
...
POKE POKE
I HAVEN'T TURNED TO LOOK!!
I'm supposed to turn my head and hit your finger!
You're breaking the rules with all that poking!
SMAK
YOU'RE PITIFUL.
AND TOO YOUNG TO BE SO HORNY!
LISTEN TO ME!
HERE ARE TWO TICKETS TO MY CONCERT.
7/25
PM 6:30 OPEN
PM 7:30 START
SO?
SO IT STARTS AT 7:30 TONIGHT.
INVITE HER.
FWIP FWIP
HUH?!
LIKE ON A *DATE?!*
TO MY BROTHER'S CONCERT?!
THAT'S NOT COOL!
WHO ARE YOU CALLING A *FOOL*, YOU IDIOT?!
STAB
YEEOOOOW!

YOU'RE IN NO POSITION TO WORRY ABOUT LOOKING COOL!!
IF YOU REALLY LIKE HER, THEN SHOW HER SO MUCH PASSION...
...THAT YOU BURST INTO FLAMES!!
RAAAAAAAH
THAT'S JUST NOT ME. I CAN'T.
GIRLS WOULD SHY AWAY.
IDIOT. YOU'VE GOT IT ALL WRONG.
WITHOUT PASSION, YOU'LL NEVER IMPRESS ANYONE!
...

UH...MY BROTHER'S IN A BAND AND...

...HE MADE ME BUY THEM.

OH. WHAT KIND OF BAND?

GLAM?

The blond one. ....

ALL I KNOW IS IT'S ROCK AND HE'S THE VOCALIST.

I'M PRETTY SURE THEY SUCK.

HA

OH...

I'M BORED. SO I WANNA GO.

I LIKE ROCK.

IIIIIZUMOOOOO!
HEH HEH
HEH HEH
UH... LISTEN...
...I'M TELLING YOU RIGHT NOW, THIS IS NOT A DATE!
IT WAS A DATE...
THERE I WAS ON A DATE WITH IZUMO, WHO ALWAYS HAD A BAD ATTITUDE.
SHE WAS EVEN SMILING!!
SORRY, KINZO, BUT YOUR CONCERT...
...IS MY TICKET IN!

WH... WHAT'RE YOU ALL DOING HERE?
CHATTER
OH, YOU FINALLY SHOWED UP.
KINZO BEGGED US.
I'VE NEVER BEEN TO A CONCERT BEFORE!
I'm stoked!
KINZOOO!! HOW DID THIS HAPPEN?! DAMMIT!!
ME NEITHER! I NEED A HANDKERCHIEF IN CASE I GET EMOTIONAL AND CRY!
CHATTER
KINZO'S SHAMISEN IS PRAISED BY THOSE IN THE KNOW.
YEAH.
SERIOUSLY? COOL!!
JUZO?! AND DAD?!
Shamisen?
THESE GUYS MUST BE THE CORE FANS!
BUT...
THAT'S TRUE FOR SHIMA'S SOUND QUALITY AND TECHNIQUE, BUT HE'S GOT ENTHUSIASM AND POWER.
DOES HE COMPETE IN TOURNAMENTS AND CONTESTS?
HE PLAYS HARD, BUT HIS STRINGS DON'T BREAK. ARE THEY NYLON?
NO, SILK.
THIS PLACE IS FULL OF THEM!!
WHAT THE...IS THIS SOME KIND OF WEIRD CONVENTION?!
CHATTER
WITH THAT VOICE, KINZO WOULD BE A GOOD ARIA.
CHATTER
I HAD SOMEONE FILL IN FOR ME ON A MISSION.
KINZO WAS WORRIED THAT HE HASN'T PRACTICED ENOUGH.
HA HA HA!
SKREEEE

PEEEEAAACE AAAND...
WHUD
CLOMP
FIIIIRE!
*DEATH GROWL
SHAKYA DEAAAAATH STRIIIDERRRRR GRAAAAH!
RAAAAAA
YAAY, KINZO!!
WE'VE BEEN WAITING!!
KINZOOO! YOU ROCK!
KICK ASS!

STRUNK
MUSIC ISN'T MONEEEY! UNIVERSE!
JANG JANG
JANG
STRUNK
UNIVERSE! UNIVERSE! UNIVERSE! YEAH! UNIVERSE! UNIVERSE!
KARMA OF THE UNIVERSE!
KINZO ?!
I'M NOT SURE HOW TO PUT THIS, BUT...
DELUSION!
BURN MY UNIVERRRRRRSE!
SELF-ANNIHILATION!
...HE LOOKS SCARY !!!!
And gross.
RA
THE GIRLS MUST HATE THIS MUSIC!!
KYAH!
I-IZUMO!
REFRESHING FIRE!

AH HA HA!
THIS IS FUN.
I'M GLAD I CAME!
SELF-ANNIHILATION!!
REFRESHING FIRE!!
GRAAAAH!
SHAKYAAAA!!
DEEEEAATH!!
THMP

BOOM

BOOM DM

BOOM DM

IT WAS *STIFLING* IN THERE!

BLUE EXORCIST BONUS - END -

Blue Exorcist Bonus Manga: Kinzo's Band Doesn't Care

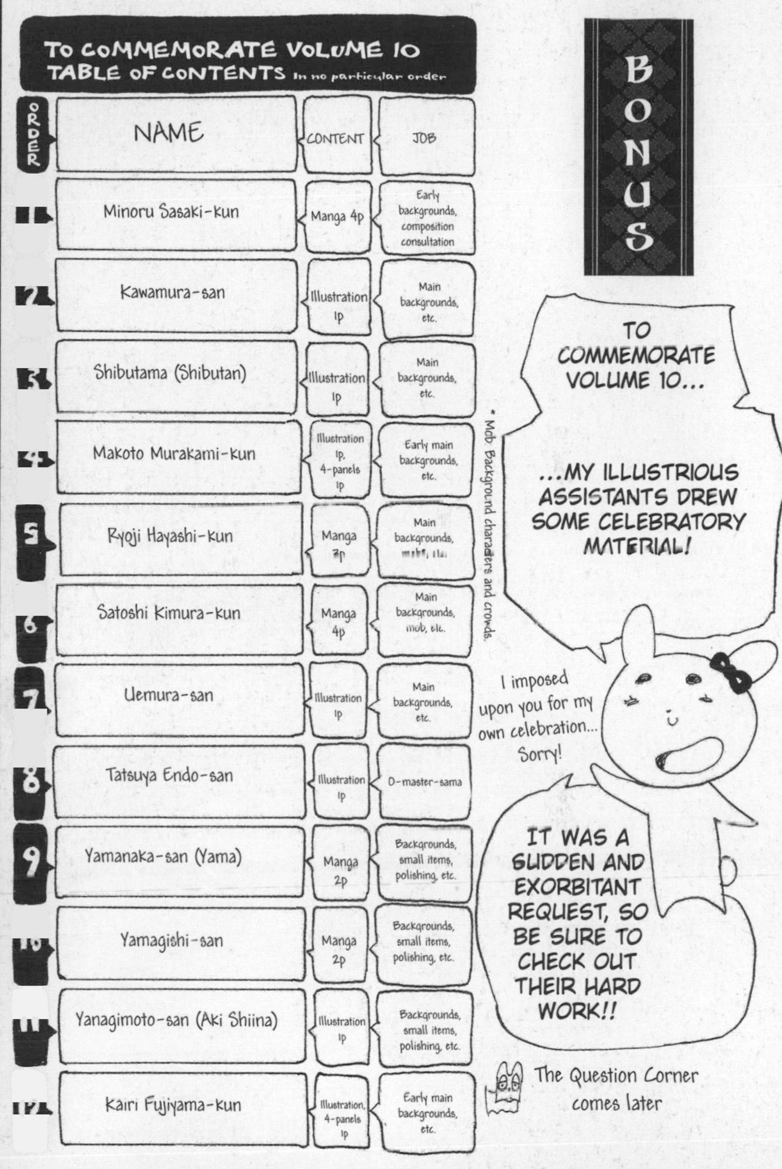

To Commemorate Volume 10 Table of Contents *In no particular order*

Order	Name	Content	Job
1	Minoru Sasaki-kun	Manga 4p	Early backgrounds, composition consultation
2	Kawamura-san	Illustration 1p	Main backgrounds, etc.
3	Shibutama (Shibutan)	Illustration 1p	Main backgrounds, etc.
4	Makoto Murakami-kun	Illustration 1p, 4-panels 1p	Early main backgrounds, etc.
5	Ryoji Hayashi-kun	Manga 3p	Main backgrounds, [illegible]
6	Satoshi Kimura-kun	Manga 4p	Main backgrounds, mob, etc.
7	Uemura-san	Illustration 1p	Main backgrounds, etc.
8	Tatsuya Endo-san	Illustration 1p	D-master-sama
9	Yamanaka-san (Yama)	Manga 2p	Backgrounds, small items, polishing, etc.
10	Yamagishi-san	Manga 2p	Backgrounds, small items, polishing, etc.
11	Yanagimoto-san (Aki Shiina)	Illustration 1p	Backgrounds, small items, polishing, etc.
12	Kairi Fujiyama-kun	Illustration, 4-panels 1p	Early main backgrounds, etc.

* Mob: Background characters and crowds.

Konekomaru Saw It All

Minoru Sasaki

SHIMA! YOU'RE BARELY IN TIME FOR SCHOOL.

YOU SHOULD GET UP EARLIER.

HUH?

ISN'T IT ENOUGH THAT I MADE IT?

N

YOU SHOULD LEARN FROM BON'S EXAMPLE.

HE GOT UP TWO HOURS AGO, WENT JOGGING, AND PREPARED FOR CLASSES.

It's about time...

THAT DUDE KEEPS HIS NOSE TO THE GRINDSTONE.

HE'S A SUPER MASOCHIST.

N G

HIS ENDURANCE AND DAILY TRAINING CULTIVATE PATIENCE AND IMPROVE HIS CHARACTER.

THAT'S WHY HE'S SO MANLY!

AND WATCH OUT, ALL YOU LEOS!

MISFORTUNE LIES AHEAD TODAY!

WARD OFF EVIL WITH SOMETHING PINK! ♡

Leo→

SWIP

Something pink.

SWIP

Something pink.

SHIMA.

TODAY, I'M GONNA GET YOUR ACT TOGETHER!

STICK BY MY SIDE AND OBSERVE!

Something pink.

AW, MAN... YOU TOO, BON?!

KONEKOMARU SAW BON FOLLOWING HIS HOROSCOPE... ...JUST LIKE A GIRL.

MR. OKUMURA...

THERE'S MR. OKUMURA.

...IT WAS SLOPPY OF YOU TO SUBMIT YESTERDAY'S DOCUMENTATION JUST BEFORE THE END OF CLASSES.

I'M SORRY, SIR.

BLAH BLAH

YOU MAY BE A TEACHER, BUT LIKE ALL KIDS TODAY, YOU'RE TOO LAID BACK!

BLAH

YES, SIR.

WHOA. THAT SUCKS.

HE'S REALLY SWEATING IT.

HE ISN'T EVEN FIGHTING BACK...

KONEKOMARU SAW YUKIO SPIT...
...JUST LIKE SOME PUNK.

A BUNCH OF LOW-LEVEL DEMONS ARE RUNNING AROUND.
FLOP
BOING

満席!?
隠れ飯
流行りの刺身
もつ
漬けもの
えだ豆
いか焼き
色んなチーズ
光りもの
ビフテキ
酒
日替わり定食
考え中
もぎたて
WIMPY FOUR-EYES SLEEPING HERE

CONGRATULATIONS!

I had no idea the series would continue for so long. I'm always rooting for you, Kazue! Take care of your health!

Mugio & Gomaji

Let's keep having fun, eating good food, playing with cats and working hard!!

from Shibutan

祝 青の祓魔師 10巻
CONGRATULATIONS! BLUE EXORCIST VOL. 10

SPORTS FESTIVAL REALITIES 1

SPORTS FESTIVAL REALITIES 2

Makoto Murakami

CONGRATS!

VOLUME 10 SPECIAL COMMEMORATIVE PROJECT!!

KAZUE KATO OBSERVATION REPORT

DIAGRAM! THIS IS KAZUE KATO!!

- Her shirts are worn-out and have random words on them.
- Her pants are worn-out, but she goes out in them anyway.
- Unlike her wrists, her toes don't move at all!
- Round eyes
  She says she can't put in eyedrops, but that's because she closes her eyes. She refuses to admit that, though.
- Her wrists bend so far you think they're broken!!

New Mexico

OBSERVATION REPORT 1
AT WORK.

HEE...
...HEE HEE HEE...

WHAT'S SO FUNNY?
OH, IT'S JUST...
HEE HEE HEE...

WHAT'S THIS? IT LOOKS LIKE POOP!

*IMPORTANT SCENE.
SEE VOL. 7.
WHO CALLS HER OWN ILLUSTRATION POOP AND THEN LAUGHS AT IT?!
KAZUE KATO, THAT'S WHO!!!
GRR!
YOU'RE LIKE A POTTY-MOUTHED KID!
WHAT?!
Seriously?

* MAYBE IT'S CONFUSING BECAUSE EVERYONE'S AN ANIMAL ON THESE PAGES, BUT THOSE ARE ACTUAL CATS.

BLUE WARS
EPISODE ANOTHER OF ANOTHER
-FOR WHOM THE POT BOILS-
This manga has nothing to do with the main manga or a certain major sci-fi series!!
SPACE YEAR 2XXX... THE EVIL EMPEROR DARK RINDA STEALS ALL THE SUKIYAKI POTS, THROWING THE GALAXY INTO CONFUSION.
DUE TO A SUKIYAKI CRISIS, FEAR AND CHAOS GRIP THE WORLD.
HOWEVER, TO DEFEAT THE TYRANT DARK RINDA, THE PEOPLE BECOME ONE.
THANKS TO THE EFFORTS OF THE YOUNG HERO KURO BLUE-MEOWMEOW, THE CONFLICT ENTERS THE ENDGAME...
MEOOOOW!
UGH! AAGH ?!!
CHECK-MATE!
YOU KILLED RIN! GIVE UP, DARK RINDA!!
IMPRESS-IVE...
...KURO BLUE-MEOW-MEOW.
SO? WILL YOU JOIN ME?
I WILL FEED YOU ALL THE SUKIYAKI YOU WANT!

NOOO!
FOR RIN, MY MASTER...
...AND MY FALLEN COMRADES ...
...I WILL RESTORE SUKIYA-
I MEAN... PEACE TO THE UNIVERSE!

CLINK
MWA HA... I SEE...
BUT WILL YOU...
...SAY THAT AFTER YOU SEE THIS?

I...
...AM YOUR OWNER, RIN OKUMURA!!
BOOM

?!

...
TRMBL
YOU TREMBLE ...
What weird movement...

MWA HA HA...
TRMBL
TRMBL
...SO SHUT UP AND COME TO ME!

GRAB
DON'T LET HIM FOOL YOU, KURO!! MY BROTHER'S DEAD!!
YOU'RE ALIVE, YUKI-WAN FOUR-EYES ?!
WHAT ?!
YUKIO?!

MY BROTHER FELL TO THE **DARK SIDE** OF SUKIYAKI!!
FINISH US BOTH, KURO!!
NO!!
IT MAY BE FOR SUKIYA- I MEAN, **PEACE**...
...BUT I WON'T KILL EITHER OF YOU!!
LOOK!!
LOOK AT THIS POT I TOOK BACK FROM THE FORTRESS!
PUFF PUFF
I MADE SUKIYAKI!!
KILL US, AND IT'S ALL-YOU-CAN-EAT!!
WHAT ARE YOU SAYING?!!
RRMM MM
JUST DO IT!
WITH ALL THIS SUKIYAKI, I'M FALLING TO THE DARK SIDE!
YOU GUYS ARE SUCH A PAIN!!
AGH!
Let's eat together!
Kuro!!
BUT... SUKIYAKI
...ALONE?
TUNK

URGH... GUAAAGH ...
MY BROTHER'S IN PAIN!
IS HE RETURNING TO NORMAL ?!
SU...
...
UNGH...
SNARF
THIS SUKIYAKI'S ALL MINE !!!
RIN ?!
ARE YOU ALL RIGHT, RIN?!
THAT'S BOILING HOT!!
GRAH! IT'S DELICIOUS !!

TAKE THAT!!
ME, TOO ?!
GAH! BLOOGH ?!!
AND SO THE CURTAIN FALLS ON THIS FIERCE BATTLE...

THE UNIVERSE RETURNED TO PEACE AND SUKIYAKI...
...BUT DISPUTES SURROUNDING GARLAND CHRYSAN-THEMUM AND SUKIYAKI STOCK CONTINUE.
END
SORRY!!
Just read it...
...without thinking!
I'LL KEEP CHEERING FOR BLUE EXO!
ATOSHI KIMURA

BLACK

I'm no help at all, but I'm taking up a whole page! Sorry... Tatsuya Endo

BRO —brother— THERS

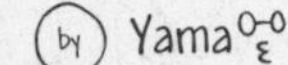

THROWING A TOTAL FIT
WAAAH!
NO! NO! YOU CAN'T HOG KURO!
I WANNA PLAY WITH THE KITTY, TOO!!
WHAT'S GOTTEN INTO YOU, YUKIO? YOU'RE ACTING WEIRD!!
Are you possessed?!
FREAKING OUT
WHOA
I HEARD SHOUTING. IS SOMETHING WRONG?
OH! SHIEMI!
I DON'T GET IT! YUKIO'S ACTING WEIRD THIS MORNING!
ACK
ACK
WAAAH!
NO FAAAAAIR!

HELLO, SHIEMI. GOOD MORNING.
What a pretty kimono!
G...GOOD MORNING, YUKI... HM?
BLUSH
SWIP

YUKI'S ACTING TOTALLY NORMAL!
BYE!
HUH?! BUT HE WAS JUST...
That's odd...
YAWN
WHEW... ROMPING AROUND WORE ME OUT...

BRO! I'M SLEEPY!
NO, UH... HUH?!
GAH
READ ME A STORY OR I CAN'T NAP!
AWWW, C'MON!!
GRB
FLOP

WHY'RE YOU ONLY DOING THAT TO ME?!
SNAP
I TOLD YOU I WOULD ACT LIKE A LITTLE BROTHER...
...SO I WANT YOU TO TAKE CARE OF ME.
SERIOUS☆BOY

NOW READ ME A STORY!
PLEEEASE, BIG BRO!
This one!
Kintaro
I DON'T LIKE YOU LIKE THIS!
GYAAAAH!!
WHSH

YAAAAAAAH!!
TMP TMP TMP TMP TMP
Kintaro

☆KATO SENSEI, CONGRATULATIONS ON BLUE EXO, VOL. 10!!
WHAT A WIMP.
He's the son of Satan?
POUT
Kintaro

CONGRATS! VOLUME 10 COMMEMORATION!!

I TREATED THEM TO TEN PIECES OF SUSHI

ART AND STORY BY: YAMAGISHI

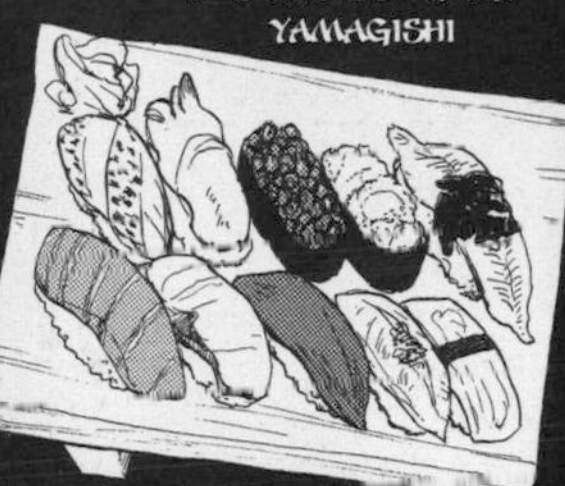

* BASED ENTIRELY ON MY OWN VIEW OF THE CHARACTERS.

CONGRATS ON MAKING IT TO VOLUME 10!

BLUE EXORCIST VOL. 10
CONGRATULATIONS
I'M EXCITED TO READ IT EVERY MONTH! I CAN'T WAIT TO SEE WHAT RIN AND THE CREW DO IN THE FUTURE! I'LL BE ROOTING FROM THE SHADOWS!
I LOVE SHIMA!!!
Aki Shiina
SCRATCH
ERO

CONGRATS
BLUE EXORCIST 10
KATO KAZUE THE MOVIE
RIN ET. AL. HELPING THE ARMY MAKES MY HEART JUMP!
KEEP PUMPING IT OUT, KAZUESAN!!
KAIRI FUJIYAMA.
WE SHOULD ABANDON THIS FUTILE BATTLE!!
HOW CAN YOU SAY THAT?
BE QUIET, RIN.
SORRY, SUGURO.
SLAM
BUT WE HAVE TO DEFEAT SATAN!!
I REALIZED WE SHOULD FORGET ABOUT SATAN AND FACE REALITY.
BUT HE'S YOUR DAD!
I'M DONE LOOKING BACK AND DONE BEING AN EXORCIST.
REALLY?!
THAT'S FOR YUKIO. I'M GONNA RUN A RESTAURANT.
NOW ALL I NEED IS SHIEMI'S PERMISSION!!
MY DREAM IS A LITTLE HOUSE WITH A YARD AND ENOUGH KIDS FOR A SOCCER TEAM.
WHY YOU!
CHEF

BLUE QUESTORCIST

SORRY FOR SKIPPING VOLUME 9, BUT LET'S BEGIN THE QUESTION CORNER!

THIS TIME, WE'RE NAMING THE QUESTION CORNER AFTER A SUGGESTION FROM YAIBA KYORAN (PEN NAME), AND WE'RE GONNA KEEP CALLING IT THIS!

THIS QUESTION IS FOR RENZO SHIMA. THERE ARE FIVE SHIMA BROTHERS, RIGHT? ONLY THREE HAVE APPEARED SO FAR, SO WHAT ARE THE OTHERS LIKE?

RASPBERRY, FUKUSHIMA PREFECTURE (14)

THIS IS A QUESTION WE GET A LOT. THEY MAY SHOW UP SOMETIME, SO TELL US ABOUT THEM, RENZO!!

HUH? ME?! INCLUDING TAKEZO, WHO DIED, ALTOGETHER THERE ARE SEVEN BROTHERS AND SISTERS. IN ORDER OF AGE: TAKEZO (FIRST SON), JUN (FIRST DAUGHTER), JUZO (SECOND SON), GOZO (THIRD SON), KINZO (FOURTH SON), ME (FIFTH SON), YUMI (SECOND DAUGHTER). LIKE THAT.

IF GOZO, JUN AND YUMI SHOW UP, BE KIND TO THEM.

I DON'T KNOW IF THEY WILL, THOUGH!!

ABOUT KARURA... WERE THERE TWO, THE ONE THAT SUGURO MADE A CONTRACT WITH AND THE ONE THAT TODO SWALLOWED? KARURA IS IMMORTAL, SO IT CAN'T DIE, BUT CAN I TAKE IT THAT TWO DEMONS NAMED KARURA EXIST? BY THE WAY, DID TODO GET MORE STRENGTH THAN SUGURO?

MIZUKI, MIYAGI PREFECTURE (20)

THAT'S RIGHT, BUT RATHER THAN THERE BEING TWO, IT SPLIT INTO TWO.

IN VOLUME 7, WHEN SHIRO WAS GIVING INSTRUCTIONS FOR WITHDRAWING THE POISON, WAS THE MAN IN FRONT OF THE PERSON TAKING NOTES KONEKOMARU'S FATHER?

IMOYAMA, FUKUOKA PREFECTURE (16)

WOW! WHAT A SPECIFIC QUESTION! THAT'S THE SCENE IN TATSUMA'S MEMORY. YOU'RE RIGHT. BY THE WAY, THE PERSON TOWARD THE BEGINNING WHO ASKS, "WHAT SHOULD WE DO?" IS ALSO HIS FATHER.

IN VOLUME 8, NARUMI AND SHISHAMO SHOWED UP, BUT WHICH WAS WHICH?

MAA, HOKKAIDO (?)

I'M NARUMI.

I'M SHISHAMO. IT'S MY LAST NAME!

THE TALL GUY WITH THE SHAVED HEAD WAS CHIGUSA. THE WELL-BUILT OLDER GUY WAS KUMAGAI.

YUKIO SUMMONED NAIADS. CAN HE SUMMON OTHER DEMONS?

MINA SASA, CHIBA PREFECTURE (12)

(FINALLY, A DECENT QUESTION...) I CAN'T SUMMON DEMONS MYSELF. IN ORDER TO SUMMON AND EMPLOY DEMONS, I NEED TO CONCLUDE A CONTRACT WITH THEM. I COULD SUMMON THE NAIADS BECAUSE OF MY MAGIC BULLETS, WHICH RECEIVED THEIR FAVOR. THE NAIADS HAVE PLEDGED TO LEND THEIR STRENGTH WHEN A TAMER WHO HAS THEM AS FAMILIARS SHOOTS THOSE BULLETS. I TRIED SUMMONING THEM BECAUSE I WAS IN A PINCH, BUT I DIDN'T KNOW IF I COULD. I WAS SORT OF WINGING IT...

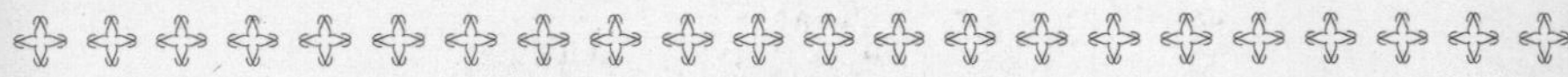

HIS ANSWER GOT SORT OF NEGATIVE AT THE END...

DID MAMUSHI HOJO AND JUZO SHIMA GET MARRIED?

BLACK EXORCIST, KANAGAWA PREFECTURE (12)

NOT YET, BUT IT WILL HAPPEN EVENTUALLY.

HOW CAN YOU JUST ASSUME THAT?!

IS RYUJI'S FATHER (TATSUMA) BALD, OR DOES HE SHAVE HIS HEAD LIKE KONEKOMARU?

CHIARI, KAGAWA PREFECTURE (13)

I'M BALD. IF RYUJI'S GOT MY GENES, HE'LL GO BALD, TOO.

SO HERE'S HOPING MY MOM'S GENES PULL THROUGH!

SURELY HE WOULDN'T...BUT IS SHIMA THINKING ABOUT USING A CAMO-PONCHO TO PEEP INTO THE GIRLS' RESTROOM OR SNEAK INTO THEIR BATH?

WANDERING EXORCIST, TOKYO PREFECTURE (13)

GASP I NEVER THOUGHT OF THAT!!

SEE YOU NEXT TIME!

※ Amaimon factoid
I've been using this body...
...for almost 1,000 years.
Old fogey!

A Full Range of Emotions

I'm not cutting corners!

Really! I'm not!!

BLUE EXORCIST 10

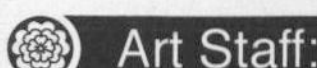

Art Staff:

Miyuki Shibuya

Erika Uemura

Yoshino Kawamura

Art Assistants:

Kimura-kun

Hayashi-kun

Yamanaka-san

Yanagimoto-san

Yamagishi-san

Composition Assistant:

Minoru Sasaki

Editor

Shihei Rin

Graphic Novel Editor

Ryusuke Kuroki

Graphic Novel Design

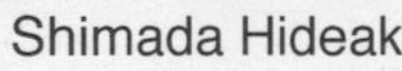

Shimada Hideaki

Daiju Asami (L.S.D.)

Manga

Kazue Kato

(in no particular order)
(Note: The caricatures and statements are from memory!)

 I'll do my best on Volume 11!! 

Kazue Kato

At last, two digits!! This is volume 10! To be honest, when I started the series, I was prepared for this to end at about volume 3.

The series has continued this long thanks to everyone who has helped bring the manga from production to release, everyone involved in the anime and other aspects of the *Blue Exorcist* media mix and, most of all, everyone who has bought and read it!

I don't know what the future holds, but if it's cool with you, please stick with *Blue Exorcist*!!

Now check out volume 10!

BLUE EXORCIST

BLUE EXORCIST VOL. 10
SHONEN JUMP ADVANCED Manga Edition

STORY & ART BY KAZUE KATO

Translation & English Adaptation/John Werry
Touch-up Art & Lettering/John Hunt, Primary Graphix
Cover & Interior Design/Sam Elzway
Editor/Mike Montesa

Printed in the U.S.A.

Published by VIZ Media, LLC
P.O. Box 77010
San Francisco, CA 94107

10 9 8 7 6 5 4 3 2 1
First printing, July 2013

www.viz.com

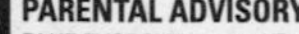

PARENTAL ADVISORY
BLUE EXORCIST is rated T+ for Older Teen and is recommended for ages 16 and up. It contains violence, suggestive situations and some adult themes.

ratings.viz.com

In the next volume...

Rin and his friends continue to investigate the Seven School Mysteries. Yukio watches as the Exwires take on the academy's ghosts, troubled by lingering doubts about his own feelings. Rin seems to be learning to control his power more, but is tapping this inner demonic fire going to be his salvation or his doom?

Coming Soon!

You're Reading in the Wrong Direction!!

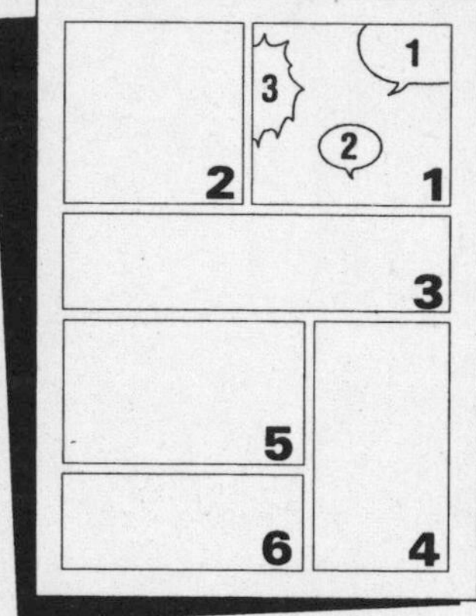

Whoops! Guess what? You're starting at the wrong end of the comic!

...It's true! In keeping with the original Japanese format, **Blue Exorcist** is meant to be read from right to left, starting in the upper-right corner.

Unlike English, which is read from left to right, Japanese is read from right to left, meaning that action, sound effects and word-balloon order are completely reversed... something which can make readers unfamiliar with Japanese feel pretty backwards themselves. For this reason, manga or Japanese comics published in the U.S. in English have sometimes been published "flopped"—that is, printed in exact reverse order, as though seen from the other side of a mirror.

By flopping pages, U.S. publishers can avoid confusing readers, but the compromise is not without its downside. For one thing, a character in a flopped manga series who once wore in the original Japanese version a T-shirt emblazoned with "M A Y" (as in "the merry month of") now wears one which reads "Y A M"! Additionally, many manga creators in Japan are themselves unhappy with the process, as some feel the mirror-imaging of their art skews their original intentions.

We are proud to bring you Kazue Kato's **Blue Exorcist** in the original unflopped format. For now, though, turn to the other side of the book and let the adventure begin...!

—Editor